5 STEPS TO A

500

AP European History
Questions

to know by test day

D1738760

Also in the 5 Steps series:
5 Steps to a 5: AP European History

Also in the 500 AP Questions to Know by Test Day series:
5 Steps to a 5: 500 AP Biology Questions to Know by Test Day, Third Edition
5 Steps to a 5: 500 AP Calculus AB/BC Questions to Know by Test Day, Third Edition
5 Steps to a 5: 500 AP Chemistry Questions to Know by Test Day, Third Edition
5 Steps to a 5: 500 AP English Language Questions to Know by Test Day, Second Edition
5 Steps to a 5: 500 AP English Literature Questions to Know by Test Day, Third Edition
5 Steps to a 5: 500 AP Environmental Science Questions to Know by Test Day, Second Edition
5 Steps to a 5: 500 AP Human Geography to Know by Test Day, Third Edition
5 Steps to a 5: 500 AP Microeconomics Questions to Know by Test Day, Second Edition
5 Steps to a 5: 500 AP Macroeconomics Questions to Know by Test Day, Second Edition
5 Steps to a 5: 500 AP Physics 1 Questions to Know by Test Day, Third Edition
5 Steps to a 5: 500 AP Physics C Questions to Know by Test Day
5 Steps to a 5: 500 AP Psychology Questions to Know by Test Day, Third Edition
5 Steps to a 5: 500 AP Statistics Questions to Know by Test Day, Third Edition
5 Steps to a 5: 500 AP U.S. Government & Politics Questions to Know by Test Day, Third Edition
5 Steps to a 5: 500 AP U.S. History Questions to Know by Test Day, Third Edition
5 Steps to a 5: 500 AP World History Questions to Know by Test Day, Third Edition

5 STEPS TO A >5™

500
AP European History
Questions
to know by test day

THIRD EDITION

Sergei Alschen
Anaxos, Inc.

New York   Chicago   San Francisco   Athens   London   Madrid
Mexico City   Milan   New Delhi   Singapore   Sydney   Toronto

Anaxos, Inc. has been creating education and reference materials for over twenty years. Based in Austin, Texas, the company uses writers from across the globe who offer expertise on an array of subjects just as expansive.

1 2 3 4 5 6 7 8 9   LCR   25 24 23 22 21 20

ISBN   978-1-260-45977-7
MHID   1-260-45977-2

e-ISBN   978-1-260-45978-4
e-MHID   1-260-45978-0

McGraw-Hill Education products are available at special quantity discounts to use as premiums and sales promotions or for use in corporate training programs. To contact a representative, please visit the Contact Us pages at www.mhprofessional.com.

CONTENTS

Introduction vii

Period 1   **1450–1648** 1
Questions 1–122

Period 2   **1648–1815** 33
Questions 123–249

Period 3   **1815–1914** 63
Questions 250–381

Period 4   **1914 to Present** 95
Questions 382–500

Answers 127

INTRODUCTION

Congratulations! You've taken a big step toward AP success by purchasing *5 Steps to a 5: 500 AP European History Questions to Know by Test Day.* We are here to help you take the next step and score high on your AP Exam so you can earn college credits and get into the college or university of your choice!

This book gives you 500 AP-style multiple-choice questions that cover all the most essential course material. Each question has a detailed answer explanation. These questions will give you valuable independent practice to supplement your regular textbook and the groundwork you are already doing in your AP classroom. The questions are divided into four "Periods" as defined in the College Board course outline. The multiple-choice questions are designed to reinforce your knowledge base, and to help you focus on the Key Concepts also outlined in the course description and included among the questions here.

Within each Period you will find question sets that illustrate the way the 55 multiple choice questions are presented on the test. A prompt—it could be a passage from a famed book, a quote from an important figure in history, a map, a painting, or something else entirely—is followed by a group of questions that relate to the subject matter. The questions may ask about different events, but remember, they share a Key Concept that ties them together. That's the kind of thinking you will be asked to do in your test—to see connections and consequences, linkages and trends, so keep those Key Concepts in mind as you go through the questions.

This and the other books in this series were written by expert AP teachers who know your exam inside out and can identify the crucial exam information as well as questions that are most likely to appear on the exam.

You might be the kind of student who takes several AP courses and needs to study extra questions throughout the year. Or you might be the kind of student who puts off preparing until the last weeks before the exam. No matter what your preparation style, you will surely benefit from reviewing these 500 questions, which closely parallel the content, format, and degree of difficulty of the questions on the actual AP exam. These questions and their answer explanations are the ideal last-minute study tool for those final few weeks before the test.

Remember the old saying "Practice makes perfect." If you practice with all the questions and answers in this book, we are certain you will build the skills and confidence needed to do well on the exam. Good luck!

—*Editors of McGraw-Hill Education*

IMPORTANT NOTE:

This 500 Questions guide will help you prepare mainly for the multiple-choice section of the AP exam. For review on the other question types covered on the test, refer to our main *5 Steps to a 5: AP European History* guide.

1450–1648

> ## KEY CONCEPT 1.1
>
> **The worldview of European intellectuals shifted from one based on ecclesiastical and classical authority to one based primarily on inquiry and observation of the natural world.**
>
> —*The College Board*

1. Which of the following is NOT characteristic of the Italian Renaissance?
   (A) emphasis on the individual
   (B) glorification of human achievement
   (C) steadfast support for the church's leading role in society
   (D) new attempts to reconcile the pagan philosophy of the Greco-Roman world with Christian thought

2. Florence was to the Italian Renaissance what
   (A) Constantinople was to the development of the Islamic cultural revival of the 13th century
   (B) Moscow was to the northern Renaissance
   (C) Athens was to classical Greek culture
   (D) Madrid was to western European Jewish intellectual life after 1492

3. One of the most prominent cities of the Italian Renaissance was not an important trade route. Its wealth was based on the textile and banking industry instead. This city was
   (A) Naples
   (B) Milan
   (C) Florence
   (D) Venice

4. What was the effect of the Byzantine intellectuals on the Italian Renaissance?
   (A) They contributed their extensive knowledge of ancient Greek achievements.
   (B) Byzantine artists emphasized realism in their artwork.
   (C) They opened up wealthy trade routes.
   (D) They used their extensive wealth to patronize the arts.

Use the excerpt below and your knowledge of history to answer the questions that follow:

"To the Magnificent Lorenzo Di Piero De' Medici:

"Those who strive to obtain the good graces of a prince are accustomed to come before him with such things as they hold most precious, or in which they see him take most delight; whence one often sees horses, arms, cloth of gold, precious stones, and similar ornaments presented to princes, worthy of their greatness. Desiring therefore to present myself to your Magnificence with some testimony of my devotion towards you, I have not found among my possessions anything which I hold more dear than, or value so much as, the knowledge of the actions of great men, acquired by long experience in contemporary affairs, and a continual study of antiquity; which, having reflected upon it with great and prolonged diligence, I now send, digested into a little volume, to your Magnificence.

—The introduction to *The Prince* by Niccolo Machiavelli.

5. Machiavelli's book *The Prince* is regarded as a definitive text on the art of ruthless, self-serving politics and the author is described, by some, as the father of modern political theory. It is widely believed that Machiavelli wrote the book with the intention of flattering

   (A) Francisco Sforza

   (B) Cesare Borgia

   (C) Frederick Barbarossa

   (D) Bartolomeo Colleoni

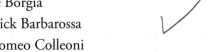

6. Which of the following best describes the political and economic environments of much of 15th-century Italy?

   (A) a few large states dominated by a wealthy landed nobility

   (B) many independent city-states with prosperous merchant oligarchies

   (C) control of most of Italy by the pope, who encouraged mercantile development

   (D) support of the territorial unity of Italy by the kings of France and the Holy Roman Emperors, who were competing for influence

7. Italian humanism gave rise to

   (A) Greek becoming the official literary language of the Renaissance writers

   (B) the welfare state

   (C) the movement toward writing in the vernacular in Western Europe

   (D) the movement known as liberation theology

(END OF MACHIAVELLI QUESTION SET)

8. Gutenberg's printing press opened the door to widespread dissemination of books and pamphlets in the early years of the Renaissance. This had a profound effect on daily life in many ways, including

   (A) allowing people to read alone rather than listening to someone recite out loud

   (B) encouraging the scholarship of Latin among the poorer class

   (C) nurturing a sense of individual identity

   (D) creating a sense of "One Europe"

9. Which of the following most clearly distinguishes the northern Renaissance from the Italian Renaissance?
   (A) interest in science and technology
   (B) greater concern with religious piety
   (C) cultivation of a Latin style
   (D) growth of national language in literature

10. All of the following reasons best describe why Poland experienced the Renaissance and Russia didn't EXCEPT

    (A) Poland was a Roman Catholic country while Russia was Eastern Orthodox and under the cultural influence of the Byzantine Empire
    (B) Poland was at the heart of the Holy Roman Empire while Russia wasn't
    (C) Russia was cut off from cultural and intellectual trends coming from western Europe by the Mongol occupation (1240–1480)
    (D) Poland was geographically closer to Rome and the Italian city-states where the Renaissance began

11. Some of the world's most widely read literary works were produced during the northern Renaissance in which country?
    (A) England
    (B) France
    (C) Germany
    (D) the Netherlands

12. According to Baldassare Castiglione, the goal of the education system in the 16th century was to

    (A) provide a practical education in construction and commerce
    (B) offer the same learning opportunities to boys and girls
    (C) phase out the study of the classics in favor of more practical "career" and technical disciplines
    (D) provide a young man with a well-rounded education including knowledge of the arts, mathematics, and oration skills

13. Considered the greatest scholar of the time, this man is credited with being the first editor of the New Testament.

(A) Machiavelli

(B) Boccaccio

(C) Erasmus

(D) Petrarch

Use the excerpts below and your knowledge of history to answer the questions that follow:

Women During the Renaissance

". . . none is found so stout of courage, so faithful to God, nor loving to their native country, that they dare not admonish the inhabitants of that Isle how abominable before God is the Empire or Rule of a wicked woman. . . . I am assured that God has revealed to some in this our age that it is more than a monster in nature that a woman shall reign and have empire above man."

—Excerpt from John Knox's *The First Blast of the Trumpet Against the Monstrous Regiment of Women*, 1558

"I know I have the body of a weak, feeble woman; but I have the heart and stomach of a king, and of a king of England too."

—Excerpt from a speech from Queen Elizabeth I to her troops, August 9, 1588

14. During the 15th and 16th centuries, some female members of the ruling classes and in wealthy merchant families were afforded an excellent education which allowed them to showcase their talents in cultural settings. One Italian noblewoman became the epitome of the Renaissance woman. She was

(A) Lucrezia Borgia

(B) Caterina Sforza

(C) Isabella d'Este

(D) Sofonisba Anguissola

15. Catherine de Medici, daughter of Lorenzo II de Medici, was married in 1533 to Henry II of France. Considered a true daughter of the Renaissance, as Queen of France she is credited with bringing several aspects of Italian Renaissance culture to the French court, but one of her achievements listed below is the subject of dispute.

    (A) She brought Italian dance to the court which would evolve into modern ballet.
    (B) She patronized painters in the grand manner of the Medici family.
    (C) She influenced the development of traditional French cuisine.
    (D) She commissioned several large architectural projects.

16. Jeanne d'Arc's primary goal was to

    (A) lift the siege of Orleans
    (B) inspire a religious revival
    (C) coronate Charles VII and unite France under him
    (D) retake Paris from the English

17. Elizabeth I is considered by many to be the greatest monarch in English history. Her chief advisor for 40 years was

    (A) Sir William Cecil
    (B) Robert Dudley
    (C) Sir Francis Walsingham
    (D) Sir Thomas Gresham the Elder

18. Catherine de' Medici ruled France twice as its regent and was an advisor to her third son when he took the throne. During this time, France was embroiled in four civil wars provoked by

    (A) the grievances of the peasants
    (B) political power struggles caused by the regency
    (C) religious conflict
    (D) unpopular economic reforms Catherine de' Medici enacted

19. Which of the following best describes the overall influence the Renaissance had on the people of Western Europe during the 15th and 16th centuries?

(A) It was a mass movement that encompassed significant segments of all social classes.

(B) It was the preserve of the wealthy upper classes that constituted a small percentage of the population.

(C) Gender discrimination became less noticeable because many women became prominent in politics, universities, and merchant guilds.

(D) The influence of the Renaissance was a factor in leading to universal education in the 16th century.

20. All of the following were reasons why Germany and Flanders were the center of the northern Renaissance EXCEPT

(A) German banking families were among the wealthiest in Europe

(B) the conquest of Constantinople by the Ottoman Turks resulted in a mass exodus of Byzantine scholars to the Holy Roman Empire and Flanders

(C) the German-speaking world was the center of European intellectual life during this period

(D) the invention of the printing press by Johannes Gutenberg in 1450 greatly facilitated the spread of humanist writing

21. Sandro Botticelli's two most famous works, *The Birth of Venus* and *La Primavera,*

(A) convey the spiritual appeal of the afterlife

(B) portray nature and humans realistically

(C) are dominated by pagan themes

(D) illustrate the dominance of males over females

22. Which famous Italian Renaissance artist worked as a military engineer in Milan?

(A) Michelangelo

(B) Caravaggio

(C) Raphael

(D) Leonardo da Vinci

23. In the late 15th and early 16th centuries, four popes sponsored some of the most talented artists of the Italian Renaissance. Sometimes called the "Warrior Pope," this head of the Catholic Church is hailed as the greatest patron of the arts among the four:
    (A) Sextus IV
    (B) Julius II
    (⊗) Leo X
    (D) Paul III

24. Florence's Filippo Brunelleschi is considered one of the founding fathers of the Italian Renaissance. His seminal work in Florence is the
    (A) Ponte Vecchio
    (B) The Gates of Paradise on the Baptistry
    (C) The dome of the Cathedral of Santa Maria del Fiore (the Duomo)
    (D) The Uffizi Palace

25. A style employed at times by some Renaissance artists such as Michelangelo and Raphael is exemplified by distorted poses and elongated limbs. This style was called
    (A) Mannerism
    (B) High Renaissance
    (C) Early Renaissance
    (D) Byzantine

26. Which Italian Renaissance architect has continued to influence architecture down the ages, including having a significant impact on American president Thomas Jefferson?
    (A) Filippo Brunelleschi
    (B) Andrea Palladio
    (C) Donato Bramante
    (D) Leon Battista Alberti

Use the excerpts below and your knowledge of history to answer the questions that follow:

Scientific Discovery in the Renaissance

"I may well presume, most Holy Father, that certain people, as soon as they hear that in this book about the Revolution of Heavenly Spheres I ascribe movement to the earthly globe, will cry out that, holding such views, I should at once be hissed off the stage."

—Excerpt from introduction of Copernicus's book *On the Revolutions of the Celestial Spheres*, addressed to Pope Paul II

"I do not feel obliged to believe that the same God who has endowed us with sense, reason, and intellect has intended us to forgo their use . . ."

—Excerpt from Galileo's letter to the Grand Duchess Christina, 1615

27. The view that was accepted in Europe until the 16th century that the sun and planets revolved around the earth was known as the

    (A) Socratic concept of the universe
    (B) Platonic concept of the universe
    (C) Diocletian concept of the universe
    (D) Ptolemaic concept of the universe

28. Nicholas Copernicus's major contribution to scientific knowledge was

    (A) the discovery of the laws of gravitational pull
    (B) that the universe was heliocentric
    (C) the development of calculus
    (D) the development of the periodic table of elements

29. Galileo helped to confirm Copernicus's major contribution to scientific knowledge

    (A) with the development of advanced mathematics
    (B) with the development of the telescope
    (C) by reading the Bible
    (D) by making advances in alchemy

30. What effect did the Scientific Revolution have on the authority of the Catholic Church?

    (A) It strengthened its intellectual authority since most scientists of the 16th century were Catholic.

    (B) It weakened its authority since more natural phenomena that had been traditionally left to the clerical leaders were now being explained through scientific inquiry.

    (C) The Catholic Church worked closely with the scientific community to develop methods that would alleviate suffering on earth.

    (D) It led to the Protestant Reformation.

31. The greatest achievement of the Scientific Revolution included

    (A) chemistry and physics
    (B) medicine
    (C) astronomy
    (D) all of the above

32. He was the first scientist to recognize circulation of the blood was part of the human body's integrated system. Prior to this, the humoral theory of the body was espoused by Galen and Hippocrates who held four substances—blood, phlegm, black bile, and yellow bile—had to be brought into balance when treating a patient. This medical pioneer was

    (A) William Harvey
    (B) Johannes Kepler
    (C) Conrad Gessner
    (D) Andreas Vesalius

33. The works of Michel de Nostredame are still widely read today. They deal primarily with the subject of

    (A) classical texts
    (B) scientific discovery
    (C) medicine
    (D) prophecy

KEY CONCEPT 1.2

The struggle for sovereignty within and among states resulted in varying degrees of political centralization.

—The College Board

34. By the end of the Hundred Years' War, the British Parliament had become more powerful because

   (A) England had become more united
   (B) monarchs needed money for war
   (C) kings left the governance of England to Parliament while they went to war
   (D) it was during that time that Parliament was granted the authority to approve or deny a monarch's request for funds

35. During periods of peace during the Hundred Years' War, English fighting age men were encouraged to practice and hold tournaments (even on Sundays) with which vital weapon?

   (A) crossbow
   (B) trebuchet
   (C) longbow
   (D) mace

36. Which of the following is true about the Wars of the Roses?

   (A) They were a clear ideological struggle between the combatants.
   (B) They began with the end of the Thirty Years' War.
   (C) They ended with the accession of Henry VIII to the throne.
   (D) They began with the end of the Hundred Years' War.

37. Which is a result of the Wars of the Roses?

   (A) They ended with the victory of the House of York.
   (B) Many nobles died, hastening the end of feudalism.
   (C) The Black Death was spread by the marauding armies.
   (D) Many saw the importance of maintaining private armies for nobles.

38. The Magna Carta exerted the most restraint over English kings in

    (A) religion
    (B) foreign policy
    (C) times of civil war
    (D) the power to tax

39. Which emerging nation-state had the strongest parliament?

    (A) France
    (B) Russia
    (C) Netherlands
    (D) England

40. Crusades were said to have gone on in all of the following EXCEPT

    (A) England
    (B) Spain
    (C) southern France
    (D) eastern Europe

41. Why was Granada, the last area of Spain to be conquered from the Moors, finally defeated?

    (A) It was geographically vulnerable.
    (B) The emirs of Granada refused to pay large ransoms to the King of Castile.
    (C) There was disunity among the Nasrid ruling house.
    (D) Granada lost its position as a major trade center.

42. What was the primary force that contributed to the uniting of Spain after 1492?

    (A) the discovery of America
    (B) the Inquisition
    (C) hatred of the Moors
    (D) Hapsburg rule

43. Which of the following states proved to be the exception to the trend of centralization?

    (A) England
    (B) the Holy Roman Empire
    (C) France
    (D) Spain

44. Which of the following is NOT a reason for the decentralization of the Holy Roman Empire?

(A) the fact that the emperor was elected

(B) a strong tradition of autonomy of German princes

(C) linguistic diversity within the empire

(D) the Holy Roman Emperor's preoccupation with struggles with the pope and others

45. Italy continued to enjoy relative prosperity through the Middle Ages because

(A) it had been temporarily conquered by the Muslims

(B) Rome remained a center of learning throughout the Middle Ages

(C) its geographic position enabled merchants to prosper

(D) it was geographically isolated from barbarian invasion

46. The mutinous troops of _____ shocked Europe by ransacking Rome in 1527.

(A) Charles V

(B) Louis XII

(C) Henry II

(D) Ferdinand I

47. Charles V was one of a long line of Austrian rulers of the Holy Roman Empire (1452–1806) from which family?

(A) Hapsburg

(B) Tudor

(C) Valois

(D) Hohenzollern

48. Which of the following contributed the most to Italy's demise in general, and Rome's fall in particular, in 1527?

(A) The decadent culture unleashed by the Renaissance tore at the moral fiber of Italian society.

(B) The Italian city-states and republics' inability to unify in the face of foreign invasion left the country open to conquest.

(C) Italy's imperial ambitions outstripped the country's ability to finance colonial wars.

(D) Papal intrigue with the French, Germans, and Spanish consisted of a "fifth column" in Italy.

49. All of the following were methods that monarchs in Russia, France, and Spain employed to consolidate their rule EXCEPT
    (A) promoting ethnic and religious nationalism
    (B) breaking the independent power of the nobility
    (C) securing control over levying taxes
    (D) establishing a close but dominant relationship with the Christian Church in their lands

50. The major obstacle preventing the growth of monarchies in southeastern Europe was
    (A) the conquest and occupation of that part of Europe by the Ottoman Turks
    (B) the patriarchs of the various Eastern Orthodox Churches worked to limit the power of monarchs
    (C) the low education level of the ruling dynasties
    (D) the mountainous terrain of the Balkans, which prohibited large-scale consolidation of territory

51. More often than not, which group or person wielded the most political power in Poland?
    (A) the monarch
    (B) the clergy
    (C) the peasantry
    (D) the proletariat

52. Which of the following best characterizes the Byzantine Empire during the 15th century?
    (A) successful commercial competition with Venice
    (B) declining size and strength as a result of Arab and Turkic incursions
    (C) republican government
    (D) reassertion of control over Asia Minor

53. Which of the following was NOT incorporated into the kingdom of Spain by Ferdinand and Isabella?
    (A) Portugal
    (B) Castile
    (C) Aragon
    (D) Granada

Use the excerpts below and your knowledge of history to answer the questions that follow:

Charles V and the Holy Roman Empire

". . . in many free and imperial cities both religions—namely, our old religion and that of the Augsburg Confession—have hitherto come into existence and practice, the same shall remain hereafter and be held in the same cities; and citizens and inhabitants of the said free and imperial cities, whether spiritual or secular in rank, shall peacefully and quietly dwell with one another . . ."

—Excerpt from the Peace of Augsburg Treaty, 1555

"To endeavor to domineer over conscience, is to invade the citadel of heaven."

—Charles V, Holy Roman Emperor, 1500–1558

54. Beginning in 1438, which family traditionally gained election as Holy Roman Emperors?
   (A) Valois
   (B) Hapsburg
   (C) Carolingian
   (D) Hohenzollern

55. In the mid-16th century, Charles V's empire included all of the following territories EXCEPT
   (A) Venice
   (B) Austria
   (C) South America
   (D) Spain

56. Besides religious doctrinal disputes, the major issue behind the wars in Europe in the 16th and 17th centuries was

   (A) how to divide colonies between the emerging imperialist European powers
   (B) how to contain the growing military threat of Sweden
   (C) how to contain the expansionist ambitions of France
   (D) the struggle between the decentralizing tendencies of local princes and the centralizing efforts of national monarchs

57. As a result of the Peace of Augsburg, the Holy Roman Emperor agreed that German princes should

   (A) become Protestant
   (B) execute anyone who had fought in the Peasants' Revolt
   (C) burn all copies of the Ninety-Five Theses
   (D) be able to choose whether their lands would be Catholic or Lutheran

58. What effect did the Thirty Years' War have on the German-speaking population between 1618 and 1650?

   (A) About a third of the population perished.
   (B) It stayed about the same.
   (C) Soldiers from Sweden resettled in the Holy Roman Empire, increasing its population slightly.
   (D) The population doubled.

59. The Peace of Augsburg represented the end of Charles V's hopes to

   (A) defeat the Turks in Hungary
   (B) contain French aggression in the Rhineland
   (C) restore Catholicism in all parts of the Holy Roman Empire
   (D) regain his title as Holy Roman Emperor

60. In 1640 Charles I called Parliament into session because he

   (A) needed money to pursue his war against France
   (B) became a supporter of democratic principles
   (C) wanted to change his religion
   (D) needed money to suppress a rebellion in Scotland

61. Which of the following was the most significant factor in the rise of national states in western Europe?

(A) the end of serfdom
(B) the acquisition of colonies in the New World
(C) the rise of the feudal nobility
(D) the rise and support of the middle class

62. Louis XIV supported all of the following EXCEPT

(A) the building of the Palace of Versailles
(B) cooperation with the Estates General
(C) art and culture
(D) the policies of Cardinal Mazarin

63. William of Orange ascended to the throne from which country?

(A) England
(B) the Netherlands
(C) France
(D) Spain

64. What was Cardinal Richelieu's chief goal?

(A) to destroy the nobles' and Huguenots' power
(B) to increase papal influence over the French king
(C) to avoid alliances with Protestant countries
(D) to conquer England

65. In the first half of the 17th century, King Gustavus Adolphus of Sweden played a key role in European affairs by

(A) opposing the expansionist plans of Cardinal Richelieu of France
(B) acting as intermediary between Catholic and Lutheran governments
(C) leading a Protestant coalition against Catholic Europe
(D) allying with Habsburg Spain to challenge British sea power

66. The election of Mikhail Romanov in 1613 as the new czar by the boyar council began the Romanov Dynasty and

(A) ended the occupation of the country by Mongols
(B) caused a split in the Russian Orthodox Church
(C) ended the period of instability known as "The Time of Troubles"
(D) led to the strengthening of serfdom

KEY CONCEPT 1.3

Religious pluralism challenged the concept of a unified Europe.

—The College Board

---

67. What was the reason for the conflict that brought about the Avignon papacy?
    (A) the controversy over indulgences
    (B) French concern over church corruption
    (C) a desire to bring the church away from the influence of the Medici
    (D) the desire of the king of France to tax the clergy

68. The period of the "Babylonian Captivity" was characterized by
    (A) shock at the church's extravagance
    (B) a new sense of piety
    (C) a strengthening of the church's influence
    (D) the increase of the influence of the Holy Roman Emperor

69. The Conciliar Movement got its start from
    (A) the outrage against simony
    (B) reaction against the Hussite movement
    (C) increased use of annate payments
    (D) the desire to be rid of two simultaneous papacies

70. Which of the following was a result of the Conciliar Movement?
    (A) reform of controversial church practices
    (B) movement to venerate Catholic saints
    (C) increased power for papal authority
    (D) the adoption of recommendations of the Council of Trent

71. _____ has been described as the embodiment of the Catholic counter-reformation.
    (A) The Edict of Nantes
    (B) The Peace of Augsburg
    (C) The Pragmatic Sanction of Bourges
    (D) The Council of Trent

72. After 1492 the Spanish Inquisition focused on persecuting
    (A) Moriscos and Marranos
    (B) Huguenots and Puritans
    (C) Jews and Muslims
    (D) Hussites

73. Persecution and forced conversions of religious minorities in Spain after 1478 happened under the aegis of the
    (A) Muslim rulers
    (B) Inquisition
    (C) conquistadors
    (D) *encomienda*

74. What was the Catholic Church's position on indulgences after the Council of Trent?
    (A) Indulgences were recognized as erroneous and abolished.
    (B) The practice of offering indulgences was blamed on the Protestants and, therefore, severely condemned.
    (C) The corruption of indulgences was criticized but the principle was upheld.
    (D) The sale of indulgences was justified when a Catholic was martyred fighting against Muslims.

75. The center of European Calvinism in the 16th century became
    (A) Geneva
    (B) Lyon
    (C) Amsterdam
    (D) Wittenberg

76. What was the immediate "spark" that caused Luther to condemn Catholic practices?
    (A) Pope Nicholas II's banning of marriage for Catholic clergy
    (B) a Catholic-inspired pogrom of the Jewish population in Mainz, Germany
    (C) the selling of indulgences as a means to save a soul that was in purgatory
    (D) Luther's strong opposition to Pope Gregory VII's opposition to "Lay Investiture"

77. The immediate cause for the Reformation is found in the activity of Martin Luther during the years
    (A) 1492–1498
    (B) 1517–1521
    (C) 1545–1563
    (D) 1555–1575

78. All of these vocal critics of the Roman Catholic Church were excommunicated EXCEPT
    (A) Knox
    (B) Luther
    (C) Savonarola
    (D) Hus

79. What was Henry VIII's goal when he broke with the Roman Catholic Church?
    (A) reform Catholic practices
    (B) install a new pope that would obey him
    (C) become the head of a newly formed Anglican Church
    (D) destroy Roman Catholicism and replace it with Lutheranism

80. Which of the following did Martin Luther and King Henry VIII of England have in common?
    (A) Neither wanted to split from the Roman Catholic Church at the outset of their activities.
    (B) Both wanted to raise an army to crush Catholic Spain's crusading missions in Europe.
    (C) Neither thought that the clergy should marry.
    (D) Both believed in the concept of papal supremacy.

81. All of the following threatened the power of the Roman Catholic Church in the 16th century EXCEPT
    (A) ideas emanating from the Italian Renaissance
    (B) the growing strength in southeastern Europe of the Muslim Ottoman Turks
    (C) the growth of the national state
    (D) the Protestant Reformation

82. What was Elizabeth I's contribution to the religion controversy in England during her rule?
- (A) She brought the English Catholic Church back under the control of Rome.
- (B) She reestablished the Church of England's independence from Rome.
- (C) She sided with the Puritans and eliminated all remnants of Catholicism from the Church of England.
- (D) She was responsible for expelling the Jews from England.

83. Why did France support the Protestant rebels fighting against the Catholics in the Holy Roman Empire?
- (A) It wanted to weaken and fragment the Holy Roman Empire.
- (B) King Henry IV of France was a Huguenot and, therefore, a supporter of the German Protestants.
- (C) The German Protestants had helped King Henry IV, a Huguenot, assume the throne in France.
- (D) Revenge was sought for the pope excommunicating the entire French clergy.

84. According to John Calvin, certain people were "predestined" to go to heaven. What did he mean by this?
- (A) Only Calvinists would go to heaven.
- (B) People who did good works would go to heaven.
- (C) Calvinists and Lutherans were destined to go to heaven but not Catholics.
- (D) God has already chosen if one would be saved prior to one's death.

85. The saying "Erasmus laid the egg that Luther hatched" refers to
- (A) the agricultural revolution
- (B) the Renaissance
- (C) civic humanism
- (D) the Reformation

86. "Christians should be taught that, if the Pope knew the exactions of the preachers of Indulgences, he would rather have the basilica of St. Peter's reduced to ashes than built with the skin, flesh and bones of his sheep."

    This passage was contained in which of the following?
    (A) Thomas More's *Utopia*
    (B) Erasmus's *In Praise of Folly*
    (C) Luther's *Ninety-Five Theses*
    (D) Calvin's *Institutes of the Christian Religion*

87. The Peace of Augsburg (1555) left unresolved which issue?
    (A) the place of Calvinism in the settlement
    (B) border divisions in Scandinavia
    (C) the Italian frontier with Switzerland
    (D) restoration of Catholicism in France

88. Calvinism became an influential force in which of the following countries?
    (A) Spain
    (B) Italy
    (C) Scotland
    (D) Russia

89. The most important change instituted by the English Reformation was the
    (A) abolition of the mass
    (B) rejection of the Old Testament
    (C) removal of all bishops from their sees
    (D) replacement of the pope by the king of England as head of the church

90. "That no Christian is bound to do those things which God had not decreed, therefore one may eat at all times all food, wherefrom one learns that the decree about . . . fasting is a Roman swindle."

This passage refers to

(A) errors of the Catholic Church written by a leader of the Reformation

(B) revision of canon law by the Council of Trent

(C) Ignatius Loyola's denunciation of Calvin

(D) one of the principle reasons for the split between the Catholic and Orthodox Churches

91. Among Luther's most important beliefs were all of the following EXCEPT

(A) justification by faith

(B) authority of scripture

(C) the seven sacraments

(D) translation of the Bible in the vernacular

92. The main result of the Edict of Nantes (1598) was that

(A) it led to the disintegration of the Holy Roman Empire

(B) Calvinists recognized Geneva as their capital

(C) it established the principles of religious toleration and equal civil rights for French Protestants and Catholics

(D) it led to the arrest of those responsible for the St. Bartholomew's Day massacre

93. What was the result of Louis XIV's persecution of Huguenots?

(A) They rose against him in war.

(B) They left France, causing a blow to the French economy.

(C) They formed a new French state.

(D) The St. Bartholomew Day massacre occurred.

94. Many English Protestants feared that James II would

(A) wage war on France

(B) invite William and Mary to come to England

(C) restore the Roman Catholic Church

(D) grant Ireland its independence

95. Besides religious issues, the other major cause of the Protestant Reformation and the religious wars that followed was
    (A) the political struggle between monarchs imposing their centralized rule over their subjects and nobles fighting to keep their feudal independence
    (B) the growing sense of belonging to a nation that has a common language, ethnicity, culture, and history
    (C) the growing mercantilist competition for overseas colonies between the Holy Roman Empire, Spain, France, and Holland
    (D) the bitterness that some Western European countries felt toward France for allying itself with the Ottoman Empire

---

KEY CONCEPT 1.4

Western Europeans explored and settled overseas territories, encountering and interacting with indigenous populations.

—The College Board

---

96. Prior to the Renaissance, the Mediterranean region had been the center of power and trade in the Western World as first Greece, then Rome and Constantinople, dominated the region. In the 16th century, power shifted to new trade centers, primarily on the Atlantic coast, as improved navigation spurred global trade. What was vital to the success of the burgeoning trade cities and ports?
    (A) access to deep water
    (B) a national navy to protect commercial shipping
    (C) government oversight of trade
    (D) a non-absolutist approach to trade regulation

97. Which pair of states had the most success in the burgeoning global trade economy in the 16th century?
    (A) France and Germany
    (B) Venice and Genoa
    (C) Flanders and Denmark
    (D) England and the Netherlands

98. Modern scholars have come to dispute the idea that a nautical school, the "School of Sagres," existed in the early years of the so-called "Age of Discovery." The school supposedly engaged astronomers, cartographers, mathematicians, and instrument makers to teach the art of ocean exploration. There is no dispute that those masters of the tools of exploration played a vital role in the discoveries of unfamiliar lands. Those who believe the school existed say it was the creation of

(A) Christopher Columbus
(B) Ferdinand and Isabella
(C) Ferdinand Magellan
(D) Henry the Navigator

99. All of these famed discoverers reached the "New World" of the Americas EXCEPT

(A) Amerigo Vespucci
(B) Sir Francis Drake
(C) Vasco de Gama
(D) Ferdinand Magellan

100. The Spanish financed the voyage of Columbus because

(A) they wanted to get to India before the Portuguese
(B) they wanted to get to America before the Portuguese
(C) Spanish clergy wanted to prove the world was flat
(D) the English had announced their plan to explore the Atlantic

101. Spanish colonies in the Americas were notable for their

(A) religious freedom
(B) self-government
(C) extractive economies
(D) adoption of native culture

102. The Spanish encomienda was modeled on the

(A) medieval university
(B) Spanish parliament
(C) Inquisition
(D) feudal manor

103. Which of the following terms referred to the descendants of the original Spanish settlers in South America?

(A) Creoles

(B) peninsulares

(C) mulattos

(D) mestizos

104. As a result of the Treaty of Tordesillas (1494),

(A) Spain claimed all of the Americas except Brazil while Portugal claimed all rights of trade in Africa, Asia, and the East Indies

(B) Portugal took control over parts of coastal India

(C) the British were given exclusive rights to the slave trade between Africa and the Spanish colonies in the Western Hemisphere

(D) Portugal gained most favored nation trade status with Japan

105. The reason Bartolome de Las Casas wrote his book chronicling the conduct of the Spanish in Latin America was

(A) to expose the flawed principles that Roman Catholicism was founded on

(B) in revenge for not being named viceroy of Cuba

(C) to inform the authorities in Spain about the abuses committed in Latin America

(D) to be named viceroy of all of Spain's Latin American possessions

Use the visual aid below and your knowledge of history to answer the questions that follow:

Western European Discoveries of the New World

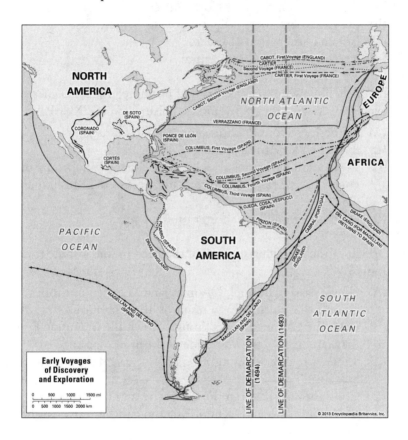

"I have already said that reason, mathematics, and mappaemundi were of no use to me in the execution of the enterprise of the Indies."

—Excerpt from Christopher Columbus's letter to King Ferdinand and Queen Isabella in his later life

106. Prior to the Age of Discovery in the 15th century and excepting the Viking settlement of Greenland, Europe's major attempt at expansion and colonization beyond the confines of the continent was

(A) the Spanish invasion of North Africa
(B) the Crusaders brief occupation of the Middle East
(C) Britain's occupation of India
(D) Russia's expansion into Central Asia

107. All of the following were factors that prompted the Portuguese to explore overseas trade routes and establish colonies EXCEPT

(A) the desire to spread Christianity to non-Christians
(B) the search for African gold
(C) advances in navigational technology either developed by the Portuguese or assimilated from advances of the Muslims and Chinese
(D) the hope of finding a shorter route to Japan

108. Which of the following stimulated the need to find a route to the Indies?

(A) Goods passing through Ottoman and Venetian territories became too expensive as a result of heavy taxation.
(B) Once the Ottoman Turks brought down the Byzantine Empire, they cut off all East-West trade between Europe and Asia.
(C) There were difficulties in traversing the vast deserts of the Silk Road.
(D) Constant wars between the Ottomans and the Mongols made the Middle East and Central Asia too dangerous to travel for European merchants.

109. All of the following resulted from the discovery of new trade routes during the 16th century EXCEPT

(A) the Silk Road declined as a major trade route uniting Asia and Europe
(B) the costs of goods were reduced for Europeans
(C) demand in Europe was stimulated for overseas goods
(D) Germany rose as a European power

110. Portugal and Spain were able to attain overseas colonies because of
    (A) their superior firearms and sea power
    (B) fair financial compensation to local rulers
    (C) treaties with local leaders
    (D) their ability to defeat England and France in mainland wars and acquiring their colonies

111. The importation of African slaves to the Americas dramatically increased as a result of the growing need for labor to harvest
    (A) wheat
    (B) sugarcane
    (C) maize
    (D) coal

112. The parallel transfer of people, cultures, animals, food, and disease between Europe, Africa, and the Western Hemisphere as a result of the Spanish colonization of the New World is known as the
    (A) Cartesian swap
    (B) Faustian bargain
    (C) Columbian Exchange
    (D) Middle Passage

KEY CONCEPT 1.5

European society and the experiences of everyday life were increasingly shaped by commercial and agricultural capitalism, notwithstanding the persistence of medieval social and economic structures.

—The College Board

---

113. The Black Death appeared in a Europe that
    (A) had already been weakened by local famines
    (B) was in the midst of the Renaissance
    (C) had been experiencing a time of peace and stability
    (D) had just experienced the Reformation

114. Which of the following did Europeans NOT believe was (were) responsible for the Black Death?

(A) Jews
(B) sin
(C) fleas
(D) bad air

115. The Black Death is generally credited with

(A) raising wages
(B) lowering wages
(C) reducing social mobility
(D) ending the Hundred Years' War

116. Peasants comprised approximately _____ of the population of Renaissance Europe.

(A) 10–15 percent
(B) 25 percent
(C) 45–50 percent
(D) 85–90 percent

117. The typical family in 16th-century Western Europe

(A) was an extended household of parents, children, and grandparents
(B) was a broken family caused by a high divorce rate
(C) toiled in the urban factories for miserable wages
(D) was a nuclear family comprised of husband, wife, and their children

118. The Medici family was best known for

(A) opening the long commercial relations between the Genoese and the Persians along the Silk Road
(B) leading the *Reconquista* of Spain against the Muslims
(C) sacking Rome in 1527
(D) being the most famous Florentine patrons of arts and architecture

119. The three orders of people in medieval Europe consisted of

(A) clergy, bourgeoisie, and peasants
(B) royalty, nobles, and clergy
(C) professionals, bourgeoisie, and peasants
(D) clergy, nobles, and peasants

120. Which of the following countries had the largest population in Europe in 1600?

(A) Poland
(B) England
(C) France
(D) Russia

121. Which of the following professions was most often reserved for the nobility?

(A) army officers
(B) lawyers
(C) bankers
(D) shopkeepers

122. "We . . . take it for granted that you will release us from serfdom as true Christians, unless it should be shown us from the Gospel that we are serfs."

This statement was written by

(A) Turkish peasants in Asia Minor
(B) English peasants under Henry VIII
(C) conquered Aztecs in Mexico
(D) German peasants in the 1520s

PERIOD 2

1648–1815

123. All of the following were reforms enacted by enlightened monarchs during the 18th century EXCEPT

(A) restricting the use of torture
(B) ending serfdom
(C) abolishing state churches
(D) easing censorship

124. Among the principle characteristics of 17th- and 18th-century absolutist states were all the following EXCEPT

(A) large standing armies
(B) development of constitutions
(C) weakening of the nobility
(D) absolutist rule based on divine right

125. "Divine right" monarchy was a term used to refer to

(A) a king's power derived from God
(B) the pope's authority over bishops
(C) the rights of subjects under a king
(D) the requirement that kings be ordained by the pope

Use the excerpts below and your knowledge of history to answer the questions that follow:

English Civil War

"You have sat too long here for any good you have been doing. Depart, I say, and let us have done with you. In the name of God, go!"

> —Oliver Cromwell addressing the Rump Parliament, April 20, 1653, as quoted by Leo Amery to Neville Chamberlain in the House of Commons, May 7, 1940

"Things will shortly happen which have been unheard of, and above all would open the eyes of those who live under Kings and other Sovereigns, and lead to great changes. Cromwell alone holds the direction of political and military affairs in his hands. He is one who is worth all the others put together, and, in effect, King."

> —John Dury in conversation with Hermann Mylius, envoy of a small German principality, September 27, 1651

126. Who was the leader of the Roundheads in the English Civil War?

(A) Charles I
(B) Sir William Waller
(C) Oliver Cromwell
(D) John Pym

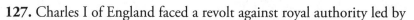

127. Charles I of England faced a revolt against royal authority led by

(A) Parliament
(B) the Anglican Church
(C) peasants
(D) French agents

128. The immediate cause of conflict in England in the 17th century that led to the English Civil War was

(A) the refusal on the part of the Stuart monarchs to raise taxes on the nobility, causing the peasantry to rise in rebellion

(B) Tudor attempts to reclaim the throne with Spain's help

(C) the refusal by the Stuart monarchs to get Parliament's consent to raise taxes

(D) the humiliating defeat to the Irish in the Great Potato War

129. Which of the following was the most significant outcome of Charles I's execution in 1649?

(A) It was the first time in history that a Parliament had voted for the execution of a monarch.

(B) The execution restored the Tudors on the throne.

(C) The execution led to the abolition of monarchy in England.

(D) England was invaded and conquered by the Scots and Ireland gained independence.

130. After 1653 Cromwell transformed England into a

(A) constitutional monarchy

(B) theocracy

(C) parliamentary republic

(D) military dictatorship

131. All of the following contributed to the growing opposition to Cromwell's rule in England EXCEPT

(A) his strict Puritan social policies alienated moderate Anglicans

(B) his growing reliance on France to prop up his government

(C) his cruel treatment of Catholic dissenters in Ireland

(D) his dissolution of the Rump Parliament

132. After the restoration of the Stuart dynasty, which of the following contributed the most to growing opposition to Charles II?

(A) his growing alliance with the Dutch

(B) his conversion to Calvinism midway through his rule

(C) his inability to establish a rival commercial center in London

(D) his growing admiration for Catholicism and Louis XIV

133. Which of the following is the most significant result of the Glorious Revolution of 1688 and the English Bill of Rights?

(A) The United Kingdom was formed.

(B) Equal rights and political representation were extended to subjects of the Crown in the English colonies.

(C) Limited monarchy was firmly established in England.

(D) England became the dominant European power until 1870.

134. William and Mary were required to accept the _____ before taking the throne.

(A) Levellers

(B) Magna Carta

(C) English Bill of Rights

(D) Long Parliament

135. Which of the following is an accurate characterization of England in the period from 1688 to 1715?

(A) a Puritan theocracy

(B) an absolute monarchy

(C) a democracy practicing religious toleration

(D) a constitutional monarchy controlled by an aristocratic oligarchy

136. After 1688, England forbade Catholics in _____ from sitting in Parliament, teaching, purchasing land, and exporting anything except agricultural goods to England.

(A) Scotland

(B) Ireland

(C) France

(D) Wales

137. Which of the following stipulated that no Catholic could be king of England?

(A) Solemn League and Covenant

(B) Act of Settlement

(C) Petition of Right

(D) English Bill of Rights

138. The most serious problem confronting Poland in the 18th century was

(A) the end of serfdom
(B) Swedish expansionism after the death of Charles XII
(C) resurgence of the Ottoman Empire
(D) weak central government

139. Which of the following combination of states blocked Russian expansion during the 16th and 17th centuries?

(A) Sweden, Poland, Ottoman Empire
(B) Holland, England, Holy Roman Empire
(C) Ottoman Empire, Persia, Hungary
(D) Sweden, England, France

140. Between the 15th and 18th centuries, Ukraine became a focal point in the struggle between

(A) Lithuania and Belarus
(B) Latvia and Russia
(C) Estonia and Sweden
(D) Russia and Poland

Use the excerpts below and your knowledge of history to answer the questions that follow:

The Haitian Revolution

"It is not a circumstantial freedom conceded to ourselves alone that we want. It is the absolute adoption of the principle that any man born red, black or white cannot be the property of his like."

—Toussaint L'Ouverture, December 25, 1799

"They have in me struck down but the trunk of the tree; the roots are many and deep—they will shoot up again!"

—Toussaint L'Ouverture, upon being taken captive in 1804 by the French general Charles Leclerc

141. At the onset of the Haitian Revolution, approximately what percentage of the population were black slaves?
(A) 65
(B) 30
(C) 90
(D) 80

142. The initial unrest in Haiti, which led to the Haitian Revolution, was caused by the discontent of the
(A) slaves
(B) yellows (free mulattoes)
(C) maroons (escaped slaves)
(D) European colonists

143. After the Haitian Revolution, the Haitian economy struggled. This was in part because
(A) the United States, fearing the slaves' revolt would spread to its shores, refused to trade with Haiti
(B) many European countries treated Haiti with hostility because it was a nation of freed slaves
(C) the demand for sugar in the international community fell dramatically
(D) continued wars with neighboring islands made it hard for Haiti to concentrate on its agriculture

144. All of the following were reforms of Joseph II EXCEPT

    (A) totally abolishing serfdom

    (B) granting universal suffrage

    (C) granting freedom of the press

    (D) granting religious freedom except for minor sects

145. One common concern of both Maria Theresa and Joseph II was

    (A) providing state social services to the needy

    (B) granting autonomy to the various ethnic groups in the Austrian Empire

    (C) industrializing the country

    (D) centralizing power

146. Joseph's "Germanization" of the Austrian Empire led to

    (A) growing nationalism among the non-German population

    (B) unification with Prussia

    (C) conflicts with Poland

    (D) conflict with Prussia

147. Why did Frederick the Great of Prussia only abolish serfdom on crown lands and not the lands held by the Junkers?

    (A) The Junkers didn't possess serfs because they were a military caste.

    (B) He wanted to keep the loyalty of the Junkers.

    (C) Eighty-five percent of Prussia's serfs lived on crown lands.

    (D) He thought it was immoral for the monarchy to keep peasants in serfdom.

148. All of the following are reasons why enlightened reform was limited in Prussia EXCEPT

    (A) Frederick was a mediocre leader with limited intelligence and ambition

    (B) political centralization had already been achieved by Frederick's predecessors

    (C) the Lutheran Church was already subordinated to the state

    (D) the relatively few burghers were heavily dependent on the crown

149. What two major events limited the scope of Catherine's reforms in Russia?

(A) the Pugachev Rebellion and the French Revolution

(B) the wars against the Ottoman Empire and the partitions of Poland

(C) the Pugachev Rebellion and Catherine's active social life

(D) the American and French Revolutions

150. Catherine's foreign policy achievements were

(A) expanding Russia's control over Central Asia

(B) gaining control of the Crimean Peninsula and the Black Sea and expanding westward at the expense of Poland

(C) entering into an alliance with China that deterred the Ottoman Empire from starting a war with Russia

(D) defeating Sweden in the Great Northern War

151. European Jews benefited the most from which enlightened despot?

(A) Louis XVI

(B) Frederick the Great

(C) Joseph II

(D) Philip II

152. As a result of the Pugachev Rebellion,

(A) Catherine abolished serfdom in Russia

(B) serfdom in Russia was strengthened to almost slave status and expanded into Ukraine

(C) St. Petersburg was sacked and Peter III was murdered

(D) the Ottoman Turks invaded Russia and recaptured Odessa and Sevastopol

153. Overall, the reforms of the enlightened despots

(A) were not able to take hold because of limited support among the nobility

(B) paved the way for democratic systems and the welfare state

(C) led to a counterreaction and the return of absolutist rule all over Europe

(D) led to the feudalization of Europe

154. Which of the following best illustrates Louis XIV's strong belief in national unity under the leadership of a strong monarch?
(A) He revoked the Edict of Nantes.
(B) All social classes must pay their fair share of taxes.
(C) The Estates General must be convened regularly by the king, but the king has the final say in all matters.
(D) French Catholics should be obedient to the monarch, who in turn answers only to the pope.

155. "We forbid our subjects of the so-called Reformed religion to assemble any more for public worship."

This statement was most likely issued as a result of the
(A) Edict of Nantes
(B) Ninety-Five Theses
(C) Edict of Fontainebleau
(D) Peace of Augsburg

156. Which of the following kings presided over the decline of royal absolutism in France?
(A) Henry IV
(B) Louis XIII
(C) Louis XIV
(D) Louis XV

157. The War of the Spanish Succession ended with
(A) the Hapsburgs reign in Spain
(B) the grandson of Louis XIV remaining king of Spain
(C) Italy's unification under French rule
(D) Britain's defeat and loss of Canada

158. The term "United Provinces" was used to describe
(A) East and West Prussia
(B) Belgium, the Netherlands, Luxemburg, parts of northern France, and western Germany
(C) Scotland, England, and Wales
(D) Castile, Aragon, and Navarre

159. The partitions of Poland 1772–1795

(A) eliminated Poland as an independent state
(B) divided Poland between Sweden, Finland, and Lithuania
(C) divided Poland between Russia, Hungary, and Austria
(D) led to the emergence of an independent Lithuanian state

160. In 1713 Emperor Charles VI sought approval of the Pragmatic Sanction in order to guarantee

(A) indivisibility of the Hapsburg lands
(B) political privileges for Catholics
(C) borders between Holland and the Austrian Netherlands
(D) the dynastic union of the Hapsburgs and Romanovs

161. The most serious problem confronting Poland in the 18th century was

(A) Swedish expansionism after the death of Charles XII
(B) the resurgence of the Ottoman Empire
(C) a weak central government
(D) the Protestant Reformation

162. Prussia was able to expand successfully during the 17th and 18th centuries because of all of the following EXCEPT

(A) a series of able rulers
(B) the willingness of the nobility to subordinate itself to the crown
(C) a large navy
(D) the creation of an army out of proportion to the size of the state

163. The establishment and growth of St. Petersburg during the 18th century was part of Peter the Great's attempt to do which of the following?

(A) strengthen his alliance with the Baltic states
(B) remake Russian institutions to be as effective as those in western Europe
(C) discourage Russian expansion farther eastward into Asia
(D) move Russia's capital out of Kiev away from Poland

164. During the 18th century, Russia expanded in Europe primarily by gaining territory from

(A) Austria
(B) the Ottoman Empire
(C) Poland
(D) Sweden

165. The nobility of _____ prevented both absolutism and parliamentary government, which eventually led to its downfall.

(A) Prussia
(B) Russia
(C) Poland
(D) Austria

166. Sweden's rise to power in Europe was marked by the end of

(A) the Thirty Years' War
(B) the Great Northern War
(C) the War of the Spanish Succession
(D) King Charles XII's death

167. Frederick I (1701–1713) became king of Prussia during the

(A) War of the Spanish Succession
(B) Seven Years' War
(C) French Revolution
(D) English Civil War

168. Between the 15th and 18th centuries, Ukraine became a focal point in the struggle between

(A) Russia and Poland
(B) Lithuania and Belarus
(C) Latvia and Russia
(D) Prussia and Poland

169. Peter the Great's reforms in large measure were determined by

(A) his inner circle of foreign advisors
(B) the needs of the Russian war efforts against the Swedes and Turks
(C) the needs of the Russian Orthodox Church
(D) pressure from Poland

170. Although he was unable to secure the final victory in the Great Northern War, Charles XII won a great victory at the

(A) Battle of Poltava
(B) Battle of Kursk
(C) Battle of Stockholm
(D) Battle of Narva

171. The ideals of the French Revolution were best expressed in the phrase

(A) nobility, power, aristocracy
(B) equality, humanity, godliness
(C) liberty, equality, fraternity
(D) justice, honor, socialism

172. All of the following called for serious fiscal reform to ease the debt crisis in France prior to the revolution in 1789 EXCEPT

(A) Necker
(B) Maupeou
(C) Calonne
(D) Lemaire

173. Voting in the Estates General was traditionally

(A) based on the principle of one person/one vote
(B) done by estate
(C) in the form of a national referendum
(D) the exclusive reserve of the nobility

174. The Declaration of the Rights of Man and Citizen proclaimed all of the following EXCEPT

(A) the emancipation of women
(B) an elective legislature
(C) protection of rights of property
(D) religious toleration

175. The Bastille in Paris was stormed on July 14, 1789,

(A) in order to capture the royal family
(B) to free the Marquis de Lafayette
(C) to arrest refractory priests opposing the revolution
(D) to seize arms to defend against royal reprisals

176. The Woman's March on Versailles on October 4, 1789, was a crucial turning point in the French Revolution because it

(A) brought the king and assembly back to Paris

(B) was embraced and supported by the king and queen

(C) was a peace offering to the monarchy after the storming of the Bastille

(D) forced the renunciation of feudal privileges

177. The term "émigrés" was used to describe

(A) nobles who stayed in France to fight against the revolution

(B) supporters of the revolution who came from other countries

(C) members of mobs in the Paris streets

(D) nobles who fled France

178. The last of these nations to go war with France during the time of the French Revolution was

(A) Austria

(B) Great Britain

(C) Russia

(D) Holland

179. Each of the following contributed to the inability of the anti-French alliance to defeat France EXCEPT

(A) Prussia and Austria were more preoccupied with the partitions of Poland

(B) Britain's military strength was mostly concentrated in the navy

(C) the revolutionary zeal of the French forces

(D) mass desertions from the anti-French coalition

180. The largest portion of France's pre-1789 debt came from

(A) expenditures on the royal court

(B) costs of welfare programs

(C) military expenditures

(D) costs for developing infrastructure (roads, bridges, canals, ports)

181. Delegates of the Third Estate were given legitimate authority equal to that of the king by the power of

    (A) the Tennis Court Oath

    (B) the Réveillon riots

    (C) the guillotine

    (D) the National Assembly

182. The meeting of the National Convention from December 1972 to January 1973 was for what primary purpose?

    (A) to establish the first constitution in France's history

    (B) to conduct a trial and pass a judgment of execution on Louis XVI

    (C) to storm the Tuileries

    (D) to abolish Feudalism and any type of hierarchy with positions based on heredity and titles

183. The Civil Constitution of the Clergy

    (A) placed the French Catholic Church under state control

    (B) abolished the Catholic Church in France

    (C) made Catholicism the official religion in France

    (D) made the clergy part of the Third Estate

184. All of the following measures were taken against the Catholic Church in France by the National Assembly EXCEPT

    (A) the clergy were forced to take a loyalty oath to the state

    (B) the priests and bishops were to be elected by all French eligible to vote, including atheists, Protestants, and Jews

    (C) the independence of the church was taken away and put under the jurisdiction of the Roman Catholic pope

    (D) church lands were confiscated and sold to those who could afford it

185. The Constitution of 1791

    (A) abolished the monarchy

    (B) established a constitutional monarchy

    (C) gave the vote to all citizens

    (D) reestablished the old provinces

186. During the Reign of Terror, Robespierre tried to

(A) execute all French nobles

(B) restore the Catholic Church

(C) crush all opposition to the revolution

(D) sign a separate peace treaty with countries fighting against France

187. Besides the violence, how was the Jacobin phase of the revolution more radical than the previous National Assembly phase?

(A) The Jacobins called for universal male suffrage and an end to all forms of monarchy.

(B) The Jacobins called for the elimination of private property and the redistribution of wealth.

(C) The Jacobins called for women of talent to hold key government positions.

(D) The Jacobins called for the abolition of all borders for a united Europe.

188. Which of the following figures from the revolutionary era was famous for his libertine sexuality and blasphemy?

(A) Napoleon Bonaparte

(B) Marquis de Sade

(C) Maximilien Robespierre

(D) Jacques Necker

189. Which of the following best explains the attitude of many European monarchs toward the French Revolution?

(A) Since the revolution was strictly the internal affair of the French government, European monarchs paid little attention.

(B) Many rushed to aid Louis XVI.

(C) On the one hand they welcomed anything that would weaken France's position; on the other, they feared the revolution spreading to their countries.

(D) Many felt that it was time that radical reform came to France; therefore, they supported the revolution.

190. Which of the following classes, through its demands for universal male suffrage and its violent street tactics, kept the revolution moving in a more radical phase?

(A) the peasants

(B) the Parisian sansculottes

(C) rank-and-file soldiers in the army

(D) the émigrés

191. Which of the following classes was the "muscle of the revolution" from 1789 to 1799?

(A) the bourgeoisie

(B) the nobility

(C) the sans-culottes

(D) the royal family

192. Which French colony was inspired by and used the instability of the revolution to declare and eventually gain its independence?

(A) Haiti

(B) Algeria

(C) Guadeloupe

(D) French Guiana

193. Which of the following events contributed to the radicalization of the French Revolution?

(A) the September Massacres

(B) the execution of Louis XVI

(C) the storming of the Tuileries

(D) all of the above

194. The majority of victims of the Reign of Terror were

(A) nobles and clergy

(B) the bourgeoisie

(C) foreign enemies

(D) the peasants and laboring classes

195. What became apparent after the Directory asked Napoleon to suppress pro-Royalist sympathizers in 1797?

(A) Pro-Royalist sympathizers lost their final battle to try to turn the clock back in France to 1789.

(B) The Directory came to rely more and more on the army for its power.

(C) France was vulnerable to foreign enemies since the army was asked to establish order within France.

(D) all of the above

196. All of the following were reasons why Napoleon was extremely popular in France from 1799 to 1804 EXCEPT

(A) he made peace with the French Catholic Church

(B) he voted against the execution of Louis XVI in 1793

(C) he granted amnesty to émigrés if they returned to France and were loyal to the new government

(D) he was an outstanding and very successful military commander

197. On December 2, 1804, Napoleon Bonaparte

(A) swore loyalty to the Tennis Court Oath

(B) called for the execution of Louis XVI

(C) orchestrated a coup d'etat that overthrew the Directory

(D) crowned himself emperor of France

198. Czar Alexander I's most successful strategy in countering Napoleon's invasion of Russia was to

(A) stand and fight at the Neman River

(B) surrender St. Petersburg

(C) make a stand in front of Moscow

(D) retreat and destroy food supplies

199. Napoleon's social origins were

(A) Parisian sansculottes

(B) Girondin bourgeois

(C) Corsican noble

(D) Burgundian peasant

200. The Napoleonic Code, enacted by Bonaparte in 1804, did all of the following EXCEPT

(A) create laws that favored business and private enterprise
(B) reaffirm the patriarchal nature of the traditional family
(C) grant special privileges to the aristocracy
(D) form a basis for civil law copied in many countries

201. To strangle the British economy, Napoleon imposed an economic blockade on his rival called

(A) the Napoleonic Code
(B) the Bastille Embargo
(C) the Continental System
(D) Anti-British Economic Policy

202. Napoleon's costliest defeat in terms of naval dominance came

(A) against the Russians
(B) at the Battle of Trafalgar
(C) at Waterloo
(D) at the Battle of Austerlitz

203. The issue that precipitated a split between Napoleon and Czar Alexander I that eventually led to war was

(A) Alexander's refusal to allow his daughter to marry Napoleon
(B) Russia's backing out of the Continental System
(C) a quarrel between France and Russia over how to partition Finland
(D) a promise by Prussia and Austria to Russia that they would give up their Polish possessions in exchange for Russia leaving the Continental System

204. Which of the following countries was the biggest supporter of Napoleon and why?

(A) Spain was the biggest supporter because Spaniards welcomed Napoleon's moves to limit the Catholic Church's grip on all aspects of Spanish society.

(B) Austria was the biggest supporter because Francis I offered Napoleon his daughter Maria Louise in marriage, cementing an alliance between the Bonapartes and Hapsburgs that lasted until 1914.

(C) Poland was the biggest supporter because Napoleon offered the Poles hope of autonomy or independence by creating the Duchy of Warsaw.

(D) Russia was the biggest supporter because Napoleon offered Alexander the title of Emperor of the East, and they both shared a dislike for the British.

205. Overall, the general goal of the allies at the Congress of Vienna was to

(A) spread the revolutionary gains made in France to the rest of Europe

(B) anoint Russia as the new leader of Europe

(C) establish boundaries and conditions in Europe to contain France

(D) create a permanent "Holy Alliance" between Austria, Prussia, Russia, and Great Britain

---

KEY CONCEPT 2.2

The expansion of European commerce accelerated the growth of a worldwide economic network.

—*The College Board*

---

206. In the 18th century, the principal economic activity of the Netherlands was

(A) banking and maritime commerce

(B) tulip cultivation

(C) timber production and export

(D) agricultural production

207. Mercantilism was principally characterized by

(A) government efforts to build a strong, self-sufficient economy
(B) the efforts of the merchant class to influence policy by subsidizing the government
(C) the efforts of bankers and exporters to establish free trade
(D) the view that labor ought to be able to seek its own market

208. All of the following were reasons why the Dutch were the commercial and financial leaders in Europe in the 17th century EXCEPT

(A) they standardized currency throughout Europe
(B) the Dutch government guaranteed the safety of the deposits
(C) the Dutch charged no interest on long-term loans
(D) depositors were allowed to draw checks against their accounts

209. The success of the Dutch Republic during the 17th century was due to all of the following EXCEPT

(A) Amsterdam banks and colonial possessions
(B) religious toleration
(C) political compromise between the Estates General and Orangist hereditary monarchy
(D) alliance with Spain

210. What impact did the British Navigation Acts (1651) have on Anglo-Dutch relations?

(A) Relations between the two worsened because the Dutch saw these acts as a direct threat to their commercial activities.
(B) Relations improved because the acts established a balance of power between the two in the newly discovered colonies in North America.
(C) They brought the Dutch into conflict with the French since France was England's biggest ally.
(D) Relations improved because the Dutch Republic was officially accepted into the United Kingdom.

211. All of the following mercantilist policies were implemented by Jean-Baptiste Colbert between 1648 and 1653 EXCEPT

(A) establishing new industries and improving infrastructure
(B) increasing internal tariffs
(C) founding the French East India Company
(D) creating a commercial code for businesses covering the entire country

212. Colbert's contributions to the economy of France included all of the following EXCEPT

(A) encouraging colonial ventures
(B) creating a national bank
(C) creating the French East India Company
(D) creating a powerful merchant marine to transport French goods

213. In the first half of the 17th century, the hub of the business world in Europe was located in

(A) Rome
(B) Amsterdam
(C) Paris
(D) London

214. Which of the following became a British possession as a result of the Treaty of Madrid, which recognized effective occupation?

(A) Jamaica
(B) Gibraltar
(C) Canada
(D) India

KEY CONCEPT 2.3

The popularization and dissemination of the Scientific Revolution and the application of its methods to political, social, and ethical issues led to an increased, although not unchallenged, emphasis on reason in European culture.

—The College Board

215. The Royal Society was founded in 1662 by King Charles II to

(A) encourage the arts and culture

(B) ennoble middle-class merchants

(C) honor military achievement

(D) improve scientific knowledge

216. Among the most important advances of the Scientific Revolution were all of the following EXCEPT

(A) the development of a vaccine for influenza

(B) emphasis on empirical research and scientific method

(C) the invention of the telescope

(D) the development of a vaccine for smallpox

217. The scientist responsible for developing the periodic table of elements was

(A) Johannes Kepler

(B) Gottfried Leibniz

(C) Dmitry Mendeleyev

(D) Isaac Newton

218. What major impact did the Scientific Revolution have on the Enlightenment?

(A) Through application of the concept of natural law to political theory, society could be governed in a more rational way.

(B) With the confirmation of the existence of a supreme divinity, the concept of the divine right of kings was strengthened.

(C) Failure to discover all of the laws that governed nature meant skepticism in separation of powers.

(D) The Scientific Revolution had a marginal impact on the Enlightenment since the latter encompassed political theory, education, and culture while the former dealt with mathematics and science.

219. The center of the Enlightenment was

(A) France

(B) England

(C) Prussia

(D) Russia

Use the excerpt below and your knowledge of history to answer the questions that follow:

"These are the rights which make the essence of sovereignty, and which are the marks whereby a man may discern in what man, or assembly of men, the sovereign power is placed and resideth. For these are incommunicable and inseparable. The power to coin money, to dispose of the estate and persons of infant heirs, to have pre-emption in markets, and all other statute prerogatives may be transferred by the sovereign, and yet the power to protect his subjects be retained. But if he transfer the militia, he retains the judicature in vain, for want of execution of the laws; or if he grant away the power of raising money, the militia is in vain; or if he give away the government of doctrines, men will be frighted into rebellion with the fear of spirits. And so if we consider any one of the said rights, we shall presently see that the holding of all the rest will produce no effect in the conservation of peace and justice, the end for which all Commonwealths are instituted.

—From *Leviathan* by Thomas Hobbes

220. What impact did the view of Thomas Hobbes have on the development of political theory in the 17th and 18th centuries?

(A) Although his ideas on absolutism were popular in absolutist countries, his atheism limited his appeal.

(B) His ideas greatly influenced the trajectory of the American Revolution.

(C) He has often been called the "father of the democratic revolutions."

(D) He would have significant influence on thinkers such as Karl Marx.

221. Which of the following Petrine reforms exemplifies the consolidation of absolute rule in Russia in the 18th century?

(A) the creation of the Table of Ranks whereby all material and social advantages of the nobility depended on serving the crown

(B) the construction of St. Petersburg and the order to all landowners possessing more than 40 serf households to build a house in the new capital

(C) the abolition of the position of patriarch of the Russian Orthodox Church and its replacement with the Holy Synod and Procurator

(D) all of the above

222. How did the Time of Troubles affect absolutism in Russia?

(A) This period had the effect of strengthening Polish absolutism when King Wladislaw declared himself czar.

(B) The chaos of the period convinced most Russians that absolutism was necessary to keep order and stability and to protect the country from foreign intervention.

(C) The Times of Troubles convinced Russians that their monarchs needed to have their power limited by a written constitution.

(D) Hereditary monarchy was abolished as a result of the Times of Troubles.

223. Among the principal characteristics of 17th- and 18th-century absolutist states were all the following EXCEPT

(A) politically powerful monarchs

(B) large standing armies

(C) written constitutions

(D) strong centralized bureaucracies

224. The Tennis Court Oath, taken by the members of the new National Assembly at Versailles in 1789,

(A) avowed loyalty to absolutism

(B) defied royal absolutism by committing to a constitution

(C) was taken only by the clergy

(D) proposed the institution of state terror

(END OF HOBBES QUESTION SET)

Use the excerpts below and your knowledge of history to answer the questions that follow:

Philosophies of Government

Sec. 4 "To understand political power right, and derive it from its original, we must consider, what state all men are naturally in, and that is, a state of perfect freedom to order their actions, and dispose of their possessions and persons, as they think fit, within the bounds of the law of nature, without asking leave, or depending upon the will of any other man."

Sec. 7 "And that all men may be restrained from invading others rights, and from doing hurt to one another, and the law of nature be observed, which willeth the peace and preservation of all mankind . . ."

—Excerpts from John Locke's *The Second Treatment on Government,* 1690

225. Which of the following philosophers emphasized the separation of power in government?
(A) Hobbes
(B) Rousseau
(C) Montesquieu
(D) Kant

226. What type of government did Voltaire favor?
(A) a representative democratic system where all classes, men and women, were allowed to vote
(B) an absolute monarchy ruling according to divine right that maintained order, stability, and prosperity in the country
(C) an enlightened despotism that secured freedom of religion and expression, kept the church in a subordinate position, and advanced the cause of material and technical progress
(D) a direct democracy where all citizens would take part in all the decision-making functions of government

227. In Rousseau's *The Social Contract*, the contract was between the

(A) government and the people
(B) church and the people
(C) people themselves
(D) nobles and the bourgeoisie

228. John Locke is most famous for advancing the concept of

(A) a heliocentric concept of the universe
(B) universal suffrage and a modern welfare state
(C) all people having natural rights based on life, liberty, and property
(D) economic justice for all

229. _____ has often been called the "father of rationalism."

(A) Descartes
(B) Hobbes
(C) Voltaire
(D) Kant

230. Which of the following called for equal rights for women in her book *Vindication of the Rights of Woman*?

(A) Maria Theresa
(B) Mary Wollstonecraft
(C) Mary Astell
(D) Mary Shelley

231. Voltaire was most outspoken and vehement in his denunciation of

(A) Great Britain
(B) the Roman Catholic Church
(C) Catherine the Great
(D) Frederick II of Prussia

232. Enlightened monarchs were LEAST likely to do which of the following?

(A) surrender royal prerogatives
(B) improve education
(C) reform legal codes
(D) promote culture and science

233. The language of the Enlightenment and the aristocracy in 18th-century Europe was

(A) French
(B) German
(C) English
(D) Spanish

234. Which of the following best summarizes the impact of Rousseau's ideas on the development of the French Revolution?

(A) Rousseau's advocacy of full participatory democracy led to France establishing a form of direct democracy.
(B) Rousseau's suggestion that property should be held by the "community" led to the Jacobins confiscating the property of nobles and distributing it to poor peasants.
(C) The Jacobins took Rousseau's concept of the "general will" to mean all the people in France must support the ideals of the revolution.
(D) Rousseau's rejection of separation of power is what influenced the Constitution of 1791.

235. What major event in Europe determined if one was a Liberal, Republican, or Conservative in 19th-century Europe?

(A) the English Civil War
(B) the American Revolution
(C) the French Revolution (1789)
(D) the Revolutions of 1830

KEY CONCEPT 2.4

The experiences of everyday life were shaped by demographic, environmental, medical, and technological changes.

—*The College Board*

236. Which of the following groups of people would have most likely lived at Versailles?

(A) wealthy middle class
(B) peasants
(C) nobility
(D) clergy

237. Nobility from what country believed themselves to be servants of the ruler?

(A) England
(B) Prussia
(C) Poland
(D) Russia

238. The major tax burden in France in the 18th century fell on the

(A) landed nobility
(B) Catholic Church
(C) peasantry
(D) monarch

239. Officers in European armies in the 18th century usually came from

(A) the landed aristocracy
(B) the bourgeoisie
(C) mercenaries
(D) the peasantry

240. In the 18th century, the peasantry constituted about
_____ percent of Europe's population.

(A) 20
(B) 35
(C) 85
(D) 95

241. Overall, the nobility in Europe constituted about
_____ percent of the population in the 18th century.

(A) 5
(B) 20
(C) 35
(D) 50

242. Nobles were most numerous during the 18th century in

(A) England
(B) Russia
(C) France
(D) Poland

243. Typically the largest expenditure item in the budget of an 18th-century state—excluding interest on the national debt—was

(A) military
(B) royal palaces
(C) education
(D) infrastructure projects

244. With the exception of Russia, in 17th-century Europe a sure sign of high social standing included all of the following EXCEPT

(A) tax exemption
(B) large cash reserves
(C) extensive landed estates
(D) a title of nobility or high position in government and the military

245. The majority of people of the emerging Austrian Hapsburg Empire were

(A) Slavs
(B) Germanic
(C) Latin
(D) Magyars

246. All of the following are true about the Russian nobility under Peter the Great EXCEPT

(A) they were forced to undergo compulsory secular primary education
(B) they gained more rights and became more independent of monarchial authority
(C) their service to the state was mandatory to keep their noble status
(D) they were given full authority over their peasants

247. Which of the following were most adversely affected by the increases in the price of food?

(A) urban workers
(B) wealthy merchants
(C) the clergy
(D) the nobility

248. The French aristocracy belonged to which of the following groups?

(A) the First Estate

(B) the Second Estate

(C) the Third Estate

(D) émigrés

249. Which class coordinated the uprising of the Third Estate that precipitated the French Revolution?

(A) sans-culottes

(B) peasants

(C) bourgeoisie

(D) bureaucrats

1815–1914

250. Which of the following was the key aim of the British Corn Laws in the early 1800s?

(A) export grain at cheaper prices to France

(B) improve the quality of British grain

(C) protect the interests of British grain producers from foreign imports

(D) set up a free-trade zone among farmers in western Europe

251. The repeal of the Corn Laws in Britain in 1846

(A) virtually destroyed British agricultural production and made the country reliant on Indian production

(B) encouraged British farmers to abandon corn

(C) was a concession to bourgeois industrialists

(D) was yet another step in erecting a protective tariff

252. The Corn Laws benefited which group the most?

(A) the manufacturers

(B) the laborers

(C) the nobility and other large landowners

(D) the farmworkers

Use the excerpts below and your knowledge of history to answer the following questions:

The Industrial Revolution

"It was a town of red brick, or of brick that would have been red if the smoke and ashes had allowed it; but as matters stood, it was a town of unnatural red and black like the painted face of a savage. It was a town of machinery and tall chimneys, out of which interminable serpents of smoke trailed themselves for ever and ever, and never got uncoiled. It had a black canal in it, and a river that ran purple with ill-smelling dye, and vast piles of buildings full of windows where there was a rattling and a trembling all day long, and where the piston of the steam-engine worked monotonously up and down, like the head of an elephant in a state of melancholy madness. It contained several large streets all very like one another, and many small streets still more like one another, inhabited by people equally like one another, who all went in and out at the same hours, with the same sound upon the same pavements, to do the same work, and to whom every day was the same as yesterday and tomorrow, and every year the counterpart of the last and the next."

—Excerpt from *Hard Times* by Charles Dickens, 1854

253. Industrialization in the textile industry resulted in
    (A) better paying jobs
    (B) the establishment of factories
    (C) improved working conditions
    (D) more reliance on silk from China

254. In which of the following ways did Britain's colonial empire contribute to the country's industrialization?
    (A) Industrial technology was shared with the colonies, thus improving the empire's overall industrial output.
    (B) Colonial laborers worked for much cheaper wages than unionized British workers.
    (C) The colonies provided a growing market for British manufactured goods.
    (D) British companies established factories in the colonies that produced inexpensive goods for export.

255. Which of the following was NOT a factor that contributed to Britain's Industrial Revolution?

(A) extensive colonial possessions
(B) agricultural innovations that led to more food production
(C) extensive and diverse supply of natural resources
(D) an effective central bank and well-developed credit markets

256. The first factories in Britain's Industrial Revolution produced

(A) textiles
(B) tools
(C) machines
(D) trains

257. Eighteenth-century inventions by James Hargreaves, Richard Arkwright, and Edmund Cartwright led to

(A) a dramatic increase in the cotton textile industry
(B) the extensive use of cottage industry in Great Britain
(C) the need for oil as a new energy source
(D) faster ships being manufactured

258. Which of the following does NOT describe Britain's enclosure movement?

(A) It led to commercial farming.
(B) Enclosure was legislated by Parliament.
(C) It was a means of collectivizing agricultural ownership.
(D) It was a process led by large landowners.

259. Which of the following agricultural innovations is Charles Townshend most frequently associated with?

(A) four-crop rotation
(B) the three-field system
(C) heavy use of manure for fertilizer
(D) development of the tractor

260. Which of the following characteristics did the putting-out and factory systems share?

(A) scale of production
(B) centralization of production
(C) size of profits for successful entrepreneurs
(D) production of textile-based finished goods

261. Held in 1851, London's Crystal Palace Exhibition

(A) showcased British technological and industrial achievements
(B) featured the opening of the first factory that produced crystal
(C) allowed the bourgeoisie to show off their opulence
(D) was organized by skilled artisans as a way to stave off industrialization of their craft

262. The Crystal Palace designed by Sir Joseph Paxton

(A) was only used for the Great Exhibition
(B) was a remarkable construction of prefabricated parts
(C) took over five years to build
(D) was the only building of that type constructed in the 1800s

263. The Great Exhibition in London that featured the Crystal Palace

(A) included exhibitions from other countries
(B) was attended by nearly two million visitors
(C) was a financial disaster
(D) only exhibited British achievements

264. The creation of what customs union among the German states in 1834 facilitated industrialization and became the basis of the political unification of the German states?

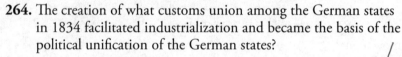

(A) the Bundestag
(B) the Reichstag
(C) the Maastricht Treaty
(D) the Zollverein

265. Which of the following leaders of France promoted public works (such as the construction of railroads) to further industry, while also supporting social welfare institutions?

(A) Charles X
(B) Louis Napoleon
(C) Louis-Eugene Cavaignac
(D) Louis Philippe

KEY CONCEPT 3.2

The experiences of everyday life were shaped by industrialization, depending on the level of industrial development in a particular location.

—The College Board

---

266. As a consequence of mass-produced cotton textiles,

(A) cotton goods became much cheaper and more affordable for people of all classes
(B) shortages of this key raw material were experienced
(C) India became an industrial power
(D) working conditions in the factories improved

267. James Watt's improvement of the original steam engine in 1769 was significant because

(A) factories could now use bulbs instead of candles for light
(B) factories located near rivers now had an advantage over factories located away from water
(C) new kinds of power equipment could be used to aid people in their work
(D) Great Britain had abundant supplies of steam

268. All of the following were consequences of the development of the railroad EXCEPT

(A) the cost of shipping freight overland was reduced
(B) markets grew in size to nationwide
(C) the number of urban workers grew
(D) coal production decreased

269. All of the following are strong indicators of the success of the Industrial Revolution in Great Britain EXCEPT

(A) Britain's share of the world's output of industrial goods increased from 2 percent in 1750 to 20 percent in 1860
(B) the nation's GNP rose fourfold between 1780 and 1851
(C) Britain's population rose from 9 million in 1780 to almost 21 million in 1851
(D) Britain's iron production grew from 17,000 tons in 1740 to 3 million tons in 1844

270. Which of the following statements is true about the conditions of the working class in Great Britain before 1840?

(A) Workers' leisure time had increased as a result of the Industrial Revolution.

(B) The standard of living had not risen significantly since 1792.

(C) Workers earned more because they worked more.

(D) Workers labored many more days a year without an increase in earnings.

271. Britain's Factory Act of 1833

(A) monitored pollution levels in factories

(B) addressed the issue of child labor by limiting their working hours

(C) provided women with equal pay for equal work with men

(D) required employers to pay workman's compensation for injuries sustained in the factory

272. The Mines Act of 1842

(A) prohibited underground work for all women and for boys under 10 years old

(B) gave women the right to work in coal mines

(C) allowed children to work in mines after school and during summer breaks

(D) called for coal mining quotas

273. The population of Europe almost doubled between 1750 and 1850 mainly as a result of

(A) fewer deaths due to armed conflict

(B) shrinking death rates as a result of a declining number of famines and epidemics

(C) less use of contraceptives

(D) government programs that provided subsidies to families that had more than two children

274. Which of the following was the only European country to suffer a declining population in the 19th century?

(A) France
(B) Great Britain
(C) Ireland
(D) Belgium

275. Which of the following countries was the most urbanized in 1850, with more than 50 percent of the population living in towns and cities?

(A) Holland
(B) Belgium
(C) Great Britain
(D) France

276. Incentives for government-supported universal education in the 19th century included all of the following EXCEPT

(A) more efficient military training
(B) religious instruction
(C) a more productive workforce
(D) the Enlightenment ideal of an educated citizen being necessary for democracy

277. "In virtue of the new dispositions . . . the peasants attached to the soil will be invested within a term fixed by the law with all the rights of free cultivators."

This decree was issued by

(A) Pope Leo XIII
(B) Emperor Napoleon III
(C) Czar Alexander II
(D) Otto von Bismarck

278. The movement for women's rights that developed during the second half of the 19th century hoped to change all of the following EXCEPT

(A) laws concerning ownership of property
(B) divorce laws
(C) the system of military service
(D) laws of adultery

279. By 1900 Europeans were importing all of the following EXCEPT

(A) wool from Australia
(B) beef from Argentina
(C) oil from Saudi Arabia
(D) sugar from the West Indies

KEY CONCEPT 3.3

The problems of industrialization provoked a range of ideological, governmental, and collective responses.

—*The College Board*

---

280. The Reform Act of 1832 in Britain

(A) created a standing army for the first time
(B) expanded the number of voters
(C) abolished the House of Lords
(D) granted the right to vote to women of aristocratic background

281. Liberalism was likely to win the most support among which of the following groups?

(A) peasants
(B) factory workers
(C) nobles
(D) bourgeoisie

Use the excerpt below and your knowledge of history to answer the following questions:

Industrialization and Socialism

"The Past has been inevitable, and necessary to produce the Present; as the Present will necessarily produce the Future state of human existence. The past has produced a repulsive, unorganized, ignorant, and to a great extent, miserable state of society, over the world, as now existing. The present, however, has been made to develop all the materials requisite to produce an attractive, organized, enlightened and happy future, for the human race, in all parts of the globe.

"Those informed know that all the materials are amply prepared, ready to create a happy future; but that to effect this result, the materials must be wisely applied, to form a scientific arrangement of society, based on an accurate knowledge of human nature. Means are, therefore, now required to induce the public to investigate this important subject, which is in direct opposition to the false and fatal association of ideas which, from birth, have been forced into the minds and upon the habits of people."

—Excerpt from the preface to *The Revolution in the Mind and Practice of the Human Race* by Robert Owen (1849)

282. Whose effort with labor unions resulted in the short-lived Grand National Consolidated Trades Union in 1834?

(A) Karl Marx
(B) Friedrich Engels
(C) Robert Owen
(D) Charles Fourier

283. Edwin Chadwick's *Report on the Sanitary Conditions of the Labouring Population of Great Britain* (1842)

(A) led to the creation of the National Board of Health, which established modern sanitary systems in Great Britain
(B) resulted in the British working class gaining the right to vote
(C) resulted in the creation of the National Health Service and universal health care
(D) created a minimum wage in Great Britain for the first time in history

284. Who of the following was one of the first to grasp the revolutionary implications of "industrialization" (a word he coined)?

(A) Karl Marx
(B) Robert Owen
(C) Charles Fourier
(D) Count Saint Simon

285. Friedrich Engels considered his and Marx's version of Socialism "scientific" because

(A) it could be proven through the scientific method

(B) he felt that through the use of dialectical materialism, he could explain the inevitability of the coming of Socialism

(C) Charles Darwin had come to the same conclusions about the inevitability of Socialism

(D) none of the above

286. Friedrich Engels's *The Condition of the Working Class in England in 1844*

(A) brought attention to the appalling living conditions of the proletariat

(B) lauded capitalism for raising the standard of living for regular workers

(C) concluded that capitalist exploitation was necessary for improving the standard of living of the working class

(D) called for the workers to return to agrarian life

287. What was the significance of the election following the French Revolution of 1848?

(A) It was the first in Europe to be based on universal male suffrage.

(B) It was the first time women were allowed to vote.

(C) It was the first time a Socialist was elected.

(D) Napoleon Bonaparte's son was elected as president.

288. England avoided revolution in the 1800s for all of the following reasons EXCEPT

(A) the government extended voting rights twice in 1832 and 1867

(B) the government enacted labor and industrial reforms to lessen the pain caused by the Industrial Revolution

(C) there was universal suffrage and an extensive social welfare system in place to help the poor

(D) the long-standing tradition of parliamentary representation

289. In his book *National System of Political Economy* (1841), German journalist Friedrich List

- (A) called for the overthrow of the bourgeoisie by the industrial proletariat
- (B) supported high protective tariffs that would protect newly formed industries from advanced British ones
- (C) believed that rapid population growth would depress wages to subsistence level
- (D) advocated a completely free-market economy in Germany to compete with the British

290. Which 19th-century British handicraft workers protested against the Industrial Revolution by smashing machines that they felt put them out of work?

- (A) Fabians
- (B) Marxists
- (C) wreckers
- (D) Luddites

291. The Combination Acts of 1799

- (A) prohibited business monopolies
- (B) outlawed merchant guilds
- (C) prohibited men and women from working in mines together
- (D) outlawed unions and strikes

292. The 19th-century Chartists

- (A) were Protestants looking to spread the faith to Britain's Caribbean colonies
- (B) favored equal membership for women in all trade unions
- (C) opposed Parliament's Factory Act of 1833
- (D) demanded universal male suffrage and political representation in Parliament for the working class

293. The buildup of the German navy under Kaiser Wilhelm II was designed to have which of the following effects?

- (A) aid the nation in expansion into the Americas
- (B) boost morale at home during difficult economic times
- (C) challenge British maritime supremacy
- (D) deflect criticism of stricter laws concerning journalism

294. Liberalism was likely to win the most support among which of the following groups?

(A) peasants and factory workers

(B) nobles

(C) bourgeoisie

(D) clergy

Use the excerpts below and your knowledge of history to answer the following questions:

The Communist Manifesto

"When, in the course of development, class distinctions have disappeared, and all production has been concentrated in the hands of a vast association of the whole nation, the public power will lose its political character. Political power, properly so called, is merely the organised power of one class for oppressing another. If the proletariat during its contest with the bourgeoisie is compelled, by the force of circumstances, to organise itself as a class, if, by means of a revolution, it makes itself the ruling class, and, as such, sweeps away by force the old conditions of production, then it will, along with these conditions, have swept away the conditions for the existence of class antagonisms and of classes generally, and will thereby have abolished its own supremacy as a class.

"In place of the old bourgeois society, with its classes and class antagonisms, we shall have an association, in which the free development of each is the condition for the free development of all."

—*The Communist Manifesto* by Karl Marx

295. Which event had a profound impact on Karl Marx?

(A) the so-called "Potato Riots" over food shortages in Russia in 1840

(B) violence on the streets of Paris in June 1848

(C) Chartist demonstrations for workers' rights in London in 1848

(D) demonstrations by silk workers in Lyon, France, in 1831

296. Which of the following was the immediate cause of the "June Days" in France in 1848?

(A) Louis Philippe's conservativeness
(B) the coup executed by Louis Napoleon
(C) the closure of the Paris workshops
(D) an elected five-man executive that was quite moderate

297. A common aspect of the revolutions in France in 1830 and 1848 was

(A) the hostility to the institution of the monarch
(B) the destruction of Catholic Church property and the elimination of it from French political life
(C) attempts by bourgeois liberals to limit the revolution by keeping the working class and its leaders shut out of politics
(D) confiscation of noble property

298. The revolution in Paris in 1848 called into question all of the following EXCEPT

(A) the monarchy
(B) bourgeois capitalism
(C) the exclusive franchise
(D) patriotism

(END OF THE MARX QUESTION SET)

299. The British economist John Stuart Mill popularized

(A) laissez-faire economics
(B) the standard factory during the Industrial Revolution
(C) Utopian Socialism
(D) central planning

300. Although ultimately unsuccessful, the revolutions of 1848 did lead to the abolishment of serfdom in which country?

(A) Hungary
(B) Belgium
(C) Sweden
(D) Denmark

301. Traditionally, society was divided into classes that often found themselves at odds with each other, a condition that this thinker defined as "class struggle." This phrase was key to the ideas of

(A) John Locke
(B) Jean-Jacques Rousseau
(C) Edmund Burke
(D) Karl Marx

302. The first philosopher to label himself an anarchist was

(A) Pierre Joseph Proudhon
(B) Peter Kropotkin
(C) Charles Fourier
(D) Élisée Reclus

303. "History shows me one way, and one way only, in which a state of civilization has been produced, namely, the struggle of race with race, and survival of the physically and mentally fitter races." This passage represents the primary idea of

(A) Social Darwinism
(B) Marxism
(C) positivism
(D) Existentialism

KEY CONCEPT 3.4

European states struggled to maintain international stability in an age of nationalism and revolutions.

—*The College Board*

---

304. The Concert of Europe was shattered as a result of

(A) the events of the Crimean War
(B) German unification
(C) the Danish War
(D) the Franco-Prussian War

305. Which of the following early 19th-century political figures was most closely identified with the concept of the "Concert of Europe"?

(A) Castlereagh
(B) Napoleon I
(C) Talleyrand
(D) Metternich

306. Following the death of Alexander I in 1825, Russia under Nicholas I became

(A) a police state due to Nicholas's fear of revolution
(B) the most liberal of the European powers
(C) a major imperialist power with colonies in Asia and Africa
(D) a limited monarchy under the control of the Duma

307. After Napoleon was defeated by the Allies in 1815, they demanded

(A) greater legislative restraints placed on the emperor
(B) abdication in favor of his son Napoleon II
(C) a regency under his wife, Marie Louise
(D) abdication and exile to St. Helena

308. 1871 was the year that

(A) the unification of Germany was finally realized
(B) hereditary monarchs, overthrown at the time of the French Revolution, were finally restored to the throne
(C) the Netherlands was created out of Belgium, Luxembourg, and Holland to serve as a counterweight to France in the north
(D) the Quadruple Alliance was formed

309. Besides turning back the clock to 1792, what foreign policy goal did Klemens von Metternich support at the Congress of Vienna?

(A) ascension of a Hapsburg to the French crown
(B) a French-Austrian alliance against Prussia
(C) Metternich's willingness to give Belgium to France in return for Austrian occupation of Prussia
(D) containment of Russia and Prussia

310. One of the overriding principles of the Congresses of Aix-la-Chapelle, Troppau, and Verona promoted by Austrian Prime Minister Metternich was

(A) the necessity to implement constitutional reforms to save the monarchs of Europe

(B) the need to isolate France and force it to be regular with its indemnity payments

(C) how to fairly distribute the spoils of war taken from France at the Congress of Vienna

(D) the importance of gaining an agreement on a collective security arrangement from the Great Powers that would stamp out revolutionary uprisings in Europe

311. Britain's policy toward continental Europe from 1815 to 1850 was characterized by

(A) a refusal to be constrained by alliances

(B) leadership in creating the Holy Alliance

(C) military aid to revolutionary forces

(D) a complete neglect of the continent in favor of its colonies

312. One of the overriding principles of the congresses of Aix-la-Chapelle, Troppau, and Verona promoted by Austrian Prime Minister Metternich was

(A) the necessity to implement constitutional reforms to save the monarchs of Europe

(B) the need to isolate France and force it to be regular with its indemnity payments

(C) how to fairly distribute the spoils of war taken from France at the Congress of Vienna

(D) the importance of gaining an agreement on a collective security arrangement from the Great Powers that would stamp out revolutionary uprisings in Europe

313. Which of the following was an important industrial city and at one time Britain's largest port outside of London?

(A) Birmingham

(B) Manchester

(C) Oxford

(D) Liverpool

314. Which of the following was a result of the Decembrist Revolt (1825)?

(A) Greece gained its independence.

(B) Charles X abdicated the throne and escaped to England.

(C) Nicholas I crushed all opposition to him and ruled like a despot.

(D) Alexander II freed the serfs.

315. The "dual monarchy" refers to which of the following pairs of countries?

(A) Prussia and Bavaria

(B) Austria and Hungary

(C) Holland and Belgium

(D) Poland and Russia

316. "Volksgeist" refers to

(A) the movement for German unification

(B) a movement for Italian unification

(C) a distinct national character

(D) war reparations

317. The Frankfurt Parliament of 1848 was an attempt to

(A) respond to Prussian aggression

(B) build the Zollverein, or customs union

(C) create a unified German state

(D) tie all independent German cities into a confederation

318. Otto von Bismarck was from the

(A) bourgeoisie

(B) Junkers

(C) proletariat

(D) clergy

319. All of the following opposed unification of Germany EXCEPT

(A) the czar of Russia

(B) the emperor of Austria

(C) the king of Hanover

(D) the king of Denmark

320. The "Eastern Question" refers to what to do with the declining _____ Empire.

(A) Austrian

(B) Russian

(C) Ottoman

(D) Chinese

321. The Decembrist Revolt in Russia happened during the reign of

(A) Alexander I

(B) Nicholas I

(C) Nicholas II

(D) Peter I

322. The Revolution of 1830 in France ended with

(A) a vote by the French legislature to compensate émigrés who lost their property 30 years earlier in the first revolution

(B) the removal of the crushing burden of government reparations stipulated by the Congress of Vienna

(C) the election of Louis Napoleon Bonaparte as the president of France

(D) the proclamation of Louis-Philippe as "King of the French"

323. How was Great Britain able to avoid the violent upheavals and revolutions that swept Europe in the 1830s?

(A) expansion of empire and overseas trade

(B) electoral reform

(C) universal suffrage

(D) rapid industrialization.

324. The Revolution of 1830 in France was just one of several so-called "romantic revolutions" in Europe that year. Which country also experienced a successful change?

(A) Poland

(B) Germany

(C) Belgium

(D) Italy

325. How was Marquis de Lafayette able to offer up Louis Philippe to the Liberals and Republicans as a "compromise candidate" in 1830?

(A) Louis spent some years in America as the French ambassador to the United States before the French Revolution broke out.

(B) Louis Philippe served in the Republican army in 1792 but was also a Bourbon.

(C) Louis Philippe had been a member of both circles.

(D) Louis Philippe had proven his Republican sympathies by volunteering to fight in America like Lafayette.

326. Which of the following was the most significant political aspect of the Revolution of 1848 in France?

(A) the number of people killed

(B) foreign intervention on the part of Austria and Russia to crush the rebellion

(C) British support for the revolutionaries

(D) the first time the Socialists play an important role in European political affairs

327. Three days of violent class war in the streets of Paris June 24–26, 1848, had an impact on the writings of

(A) Gracchus Babeuf

(B) Edmund Burke

(C) Karl Marx

(D) Georg Hegel

328. _____ transformed the loosely joined North German Confederation into the German Empire, which soon established itself as a modern state.

(A) Otto von Bismarck

(B) Kaiser Wilhelm

(C) Nicholas I

(D) Louis Philippe

329. Emperor Napoleon III of France lost his throne due to the

(A) failure of his Mexican adventure

(B) financial crash of 1857

(C) defeat in the war with Prussia

(D) Dreyfus Affair

330. Bismarck extended the vote to most adult male Germans because he

(A) was a passionate democrat

(B) wanted to copy the English

(C) was convinced conservative peasants and artisans would outvote middle-class liberals

(D) was forced by the emperor to do so

331. By refusing to support the Greek uprising in 1821

(A) Czar Alexander I forever lost the chance for Russia to play a major role in Balkan politics

(B) Alexander I sacrificed Russian national interests to stand together with Metternich and oppose revolutionary upheavals in Europe

(C) Russia avoided a possible two-front war with the Ottoman Empire and Austria

(D) Russia turned its sights on consolidating its control over Poland

332. Demonstrating the division between the eastern and western members of the Quintuple Alliance, Britain and France refused to accept the protocol created by the _____.

(A) Congress of Aix-la-Chapelle

(B) Congress of Troppau

(C) Congress of Verona

(D) July Ordinances

333. Which of the following Serbian-dominated territories was placed under Austro-Hungarian occupation after the country's formal independence was recognized at the Treaty of Berlin in 1878?

(A) Croatia

(B) Bosnia

(C) Kosovo

(D) Slovenia

334. Which of the following can be credited for saving the Belgians' independence movement?

(A) the Netherlands

(B) Russia

(C) Prussia

(D) Poland

335. As a result of the Polish uprising in 1830,

(A) Nicholas I abrogated Poland's constitution and fully incorporated it into the Russian Empire
(B) Poland became independent minus its ethnic lands in Prussia
(C) Poland's constitution was reinstated
(D) Russia took all of Ukraine and Belarus under its control

336. During the 19th century, nationalism most often contributed to the _____ in Europe.

(A) consolidation of multi-ethnic states
(B) growth of the power of the Catholic Church
(C) separatist tendencies that weakened the multi-ethnic states
(D) clash of multi-ethnic states

337. In 1878 Romania, Serbia, and Bulgaria gained independence from

(A) Russia
(B) the Ottoman Empire
(C) Austria-Hungary
(D) Greece

338. As a result of the _____, France was given permission to intervene militarily in Spain to suppress the revolutionaries and return the king and church to prominence.

(A) Congress of Aix-la-Chapelle
(B) Congress of Troppau
(C) Congress of Verona
(D) Congress of Vienna

339. Which of the following can be credited for saving the Belgian independence movement?

(A) Russia
(B) Prussia
(C) Poland
(D) Austria

340. The enchantment with mysticism among the Russian nobility, including the czar and his family, is closely linked to

(A) Grigori Rasputin
(B) Alexander Samsonov
(C) Leon Trotsky
(D) Ivan Turgenev

341. Proponents of nationalism in the mid–19th century espoused

(A) universal human rights
(B) creating Utopian Socialist communes throughout western Europe
(C) free trade to promote industrial development
(D) the idea that different peoples had distinct historical missions

342. The nationalists of the first half of the 19th century were often

(A) conservatives waving the flag of hard-line politics
(B) radicals who called for working-class revolution
(C) liberals attempting to overthrow tyrannical regimes
(D) Romantics who valued the vernacular and folklore

343. At the Congress of Aix-la-Chapelle, _____ was admitted to the newly formed Quintuple Alliance.

(A) Austria
(B) France
(C) Italy
(D) Prussia

Use the excerpts below and your knowledge of history to answer the questions that follow:

Greek Independence

"The mountains look on Marathon— / And Marathon looks on the sea;

And musing there an hour alone, / I dream'd that Greece might still be free;

For standing on the Persians' grave, / I could not deem myself a slave."

"A king sate on the rocky brow / Which looks o'er sea-born Salamis;

And ships, by thousands, lay below, / And men in nations;—all were his!

He counted them at break of day— / And when the sun set, where were they?"

"And where are they? and where art thou, / My country? On thy voice-less shore

The heroic lay is tuneless now— / The heroic bosom beats no more!

And must thy lyre, so long divine, / Degenerate into hands like mine?"

—Excerpts from "The Isles of Greece" by Lord Byron (1821)

344. Which of the following countries came to the aid of the Greeks as they struggled for independence in the 1820s?

(A) Spain
(B) Russia
(C) Austria
(D) Ottoman Turkey

345. After the Greeks achieved independence in 1832, what type of government was established?

(A) the first Socialist state
(B) a monarchy
(C) a democratic republic with limited suffrage
(D) decentralized city-states reflecting classical Greece

346. How was Greece able to get both conservatives in Russia and liberals in western Europe to support its drive for independence?

(A) Greek leaders offered both the chance to join in an anti-Turkish campaign where they could share the spoils of a crumbled empire.

(B) Western European liberals saw Greece as the foundation of western civilization while Russian conservatives identified with Greece as the country where Christian Orthodoxy was established.

(C) The Greek leader of independence spent his early years in the Russian military but later studied at the Sorbonne in France.

(D) Famine in Greece as a result of Turkish neglect galvanized sympathy for the Greek cause all over Europe.

347. The Great _____ Emigration (1831–1870) involved at least 30,000 people and was a consequence of failed insurrections against foreign occupation.

(A) Serbian
(B) Belgian
(C) Polish
(D) Hungarian

348. After the publication of Theodor Herzl's book *The Jewish State*,

(A) Jews began to immigrate to the United States
(B) the Ottoman Empire declared that there could be no Jewish immigration
(C) a Zionist Congress proclaimed its aim to create that state in Palestine
(D) Jews in Arab countries began moving to Palestine

349. The worst persecution of Jews in the late 19th century and early 20th century took place in

(A) Italy
(B) England
(C) the Netherlands
(D) Russia

350. Which of the following countries sacrificed the most territory to the Prussians in the long-term process of the first unification of Germany in 1870?

(A) France
(B) Austria
(C) Denmark
(D) Holland

KEY CONCEPT 3.5

A variety of motives and methods led to the intensification of European global control and increased tensions among the Great Powers.

—The College Board

---

351. Which country gained control of much of southern Africa during the 1800s?

(A) France
(B) Italy
(C) Britain
(D) Belgium

352. Kipling's justification of imperialism in *The White Man's Burden* is a good example of

(A) Social Darwinism
(B) a defense of native traditions
(C) scientific Socialism
(D) anarchism

353. Why did Christian missionary groups follow explorers to Africa?

(A) to gather slaves
(B) to convert Africans to Christianity
(C) to study African culture
(D) to map out the courses of rivers

354. Why was the Berlin Conference held in 1884?

(A) to stop Leopold II from taking over Africa
(B) to include Africans on plans for dividing the continent
(C) to carve up Africa between the major European imperialist powers
(D) to stop trading practices on the Congo River

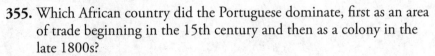

355. Which African country did the Portuguese dominate, first as an area of trade beginning in the 15th century and then as a colony in the late 1800s?

(A) Zimbabwe
(B) Mozambique
(C) Togo
(D) Congo

356. In 1875 which country bought Egyptian shares of the Suez Canal?

(A) Turkey
(B) France
(C) Britain
(D) Saudi Arabia

357. After 1908 the major reason the world became interested in the Middle East was

(A) the discovery of gold
(B) to defeat the growing strength of Saddam Hussein's Iraq
(C) the discovery of oil
(D) to start a new crusade to win back Jerusalem from the infidels

358. Which of the following regions were targets of Russian imperialism in the 19th century?

(A) Far East and the Pacific Islands
(B) North and South America
(C) the Caucasus and Central Asia
(D) South Asia

359. What was/is the strategic importance of the Suez Canal?

(A) It greatly shortened the sea route between Europe and the west coast of North America.

(B) Many oil refineries are located along the 100-mile length of the canal.

(C) It brought enormous revenues to the Saudi Arabian government.

(D) It greatly shortened the sea route from Europe to South Asia and East Asia.

360. One of the main reasons why the British were able to establish control over India was

(A) Muslims and Hindus often clashed, weakening the central government

(B) the British defeated the Portuguese and drove them out of India

(C) the Mughal rulers invited the British to rule them

(D) the Indians were won over by a promised access to British consumer goods

361. Initial British dominance of India was through

(A) willing Mughal rulers

(B) the British East India Company

(C) sepoys

(D) the British monarchy

362. The underlying reason for the Sepoy Rebellion was

(A) India's opposition to Britain's salt monopoly

(B) Indian opposition to British attempts to impose British culture on them

(C) Indian soldiers' refusal to fight against the French

(D) Britain's violent suppression of a peaceful demonstration

363. Which of the following was a result of the Sepoy Rebellion?

(A) India became a protectorate of Britain.

(B) Britain began to rule India directly.

(C) The East India Company took over the rule of India.

(D) Indians were removed from all military service in British India.

364. All of the following were results of British colonial rule EXCEPT

(A) they introduced Western education to Indian elites

(B) the British brought legal reforms

(C) the British expanded India's infrastructure

(D) they brought economic prosperity

365. Which of the following statements best describes British economic policy in India?

(A) The British "deindustrialized" India by destroying native industries and forcing Indians to rely on British imported finished goods.

(B) The British "hyperindustrialized" India, making the country the most economically advanced in Asia.

(C) The British provided India with technological know-how so it could compete with other countries.

(D) The British stirred resentment by raising taxes.

366. The British insistence that Indian farmers grow cash crops

(A) greatly benefited Indian farmers economically

(B) led to the invention of many new farming techniques

(C) benefited the British but led to famine in India

(D) allowed Britain to retain its global economic leadership

367. The major lesson the Chinese learned from the Opium War was that

(A) famines resulted because farmers were addicted to opium and therefore produced less food

(B) it had fallen behind the West in technological achievements

(C) Portugal was a strong naval power

(D) the Chinese could use opium to challenge the British

368. The most important long-term concession China had to make to Great Britain in the Treaty of Nanjing was to

(A) hand over most of its gold reserve

(B) hand over Hong Kong to Great Britain

(C) give up its whole navy to Great Britain

(D) make all other foreign countries remove themselves from Chinese trade

369. The _____ was a major upheaval in
19th century China that weakened the imperial government, forced
it to rely on aid from Britain and France, and caused millions of
deaths.

(A) Boxer Rebellion
(B) Taiping Rebellion
(C) Communist Revolution
(D) Cultural Revolution

370. One reason Germany began to fear Russia from 1900 to 1914
was the

(A) Russian alliance with Austria
(B) completion of a naval fleet matching Germany's in size
(C) rapid rate of industrialization
(D) Russian militarization of the Polish-German border

371. From 1900 to 1914 tensions arose between Britain and Germany
because of all of the following EXCEPT

(A) a naval race
(B) colonial rivalries
(C) Germany's alliance with Russia
(D) increasing German investments in the Balkans

372. "All the remaining European culture-bearing peoples possess areas
outside our continent where their languages and customs can take
firm root and flourish. This fact, so painful to [our] national pride,
also represents a great economic disadvantage."

"Our nation" in this passage was

(A) Russia
(B) Germany
(C) France
(D) Spain

373. Austria-Hungary annexed Bosnia-Herzegovina in 1908 in order to

(A) block the creation of a greater Serbian kingdom
(B) seal its alliance with Russia
(C) enable the British navy to use Adriatic ports
(D) facilitate the creation of a southern Slav state

374. Which of the following areas, which the British controlled in the 1800s, has NOT yet gained independence?

(A) Egypt
(B) Malta
(C) Gibraltar
(D) Cyprus

375. Britain and France helped prop up the Ottoman Empire during the 19th century because

(A) of increased religious toleration during the Victorian period
(B) the Ottomans assisted them in keeping Greece from being independent
(C) of fear that Russian power would penetrate into the Balkans
(D) of personal regard for Abdul Hamid II

KEY CONCEPT 3.6

European ideas and culture expressed a tension between objectivity and scientific realism on one hand, and subjectivity and individual expression on the other hand.

—*The College Board*

---

376. All of the following were major artistic and literary contributors to the period of Romanticism EXCEPT

(A) Louis David
(B) Eugene Delacroix
(C) Lord Byron
(D) Alexander Pushkin

377. All of the following are important principles of Romanticism EXCEPT

(A) emphasis on moods and expressions
(B) emphasis on peculiar customs that the intellect could never classify
(C) the importance of the subconscious
(D) the use of dramatic imagery to provoke emotion

378. All of the following were major artistic and literary contributors to Romanticism EXCEPT

(A) Jacques-Louis David
(B) Eugene Delacroix
(C) Lord Byron
(D) Victor Hugo

379. Which English poet was NOT a prominent member of the Romantic movement?

(A) William Wordsworth
(B) Alexander Pope
(C) Samuel Taylor Coleridge
(D) William Blake

380. Which of these novelists is famous for his/her historical novels?

(A) Johann Wolfgang von Goethe
(B) Jane Austen
(C) Sir Walter Scott
(D) Victor Hugo

381. Romantic nationalism was embraced by many artists, many of whom also espoused the values of

(A) Socialism
(B) conservatism
(C) liberalism
(D) radicalism

1914 to Present

382. "The Serbian Government must cooperate inside their country with the organs of the Imperial and Royal Government in the suppression of subversive movements directed against the integrity of the monarchy."

This requirement was part of the ultimatum issued in 1914 by

(A) Austria-Hungary
(B) Germany
(C) France
(D) Italy

383. The Austrian annexation of Bosnia in 1908 threatened the nationalist aspirations of which of the following countries?

(A) Turkey
(B) Romania
(C) Serbia
(D) Bulgaria

384. All of the following were contributory causes of World War I EXCEPT

(A) alliances between all the great powers
(B) the arms race
(C) Bolshevism
(D) Balkan nationalism

385. The dismissal of Bismarck by Kaiser William II paved the way for an alliance between which of the following countries during World War I?

(A) France and Russia
(B) Serbia and Russia
(C) Great Britain and Belgium
(D) Germany and Austria-Hungary

386. The Schlieffen Plan indicated that the German General Staff

(A) did not expect to go to war with Russia
(B) expected a long, drawn-out war
(C) anticipated a war on two fronts
(D) did not expect Austria-Hungary to honor the Triple Alliance

387. Russia was never a part of which of the following alliances?

(A) Triple Entente
(B) Triple Alliance
(C) Three Emperors League
(D) Allied Powers

388. The two crises over Morocco in the early 20th century almost brought about war between

(A) England and France
(B) England and Morocco
(C) France and Germany
(D) Italy and France

389. The building of a large German navy in the first decade of the 20th century greatly antagonized

(A) France
(B) Great Britain
(C) Russia
(D) the United States

390. The theater of war on the western front 1914–1918 lay largely in

(A) Germany
(B) France
(C) Britain
(D) Netherlands

391. Popular opinion in Germany, Austria, and Russia largely reacted to the outbreak of war in 1914 with

(A) horror and aversion
(B) resigned acceptance
(C) great enthusiasm
(D) fear of defeat

392. Which was the last major European country to adopt compulsory military service?

(A) Germany
(B) France
(C) Russia
(D) Britain

393. Trench warfare was established along the western front early in World War I because

(A) airplanes allowed most of the fighting to be done in the skies
(B) improvements in the rifle made snipers the principal combatants
(C) the terrain made it difficult to assemble large armies
(D) defensive weapons had gained the advantage over offensive ones

394. To break the deadlock of trench warfare, nations resorted to all of the following EXCEPT

(A) the use of tanks
(B) widespread use of poison gas
(C) artillery barrages
(D) increased dependence on cavalry

395. The British won a major propaganda victory at the start of World War I because of

(A) the sinking of the *Lusitania*

(B) the Zimmerman telegram

(C) German atrocities in Belgium

(D) the Battle of the Marne

396. Which of the following countries entered World War I last?

(A) Russia

(B) France

(C) Serbia

(D) England

397. In 1915, Italy made the decision to

(A) enter the war on the side of the Central Powers

(B) enter the war on the side of the Entente Powers

(C) stay neutral

(D) wait until the United States entered the war

398. British promises and assistance to Arabs fighting in the Middle East were designed to

(A) create their own independent countries

(B) gain enough Arab goodwill so that opposition to a new Jewish state would be minimal

(C) remove French and Russian influence from the region

(D) help the Allied war effort by denying Arab support to Turkey

Use the excerpt below and your knowledge of history to answer the questions that follow:

Woodrow Wilson's Fourteen Points

"It will be our wish and purpose that the processes of peace, when they are begun, shall be absolutely open and that they shall involve and permit henceforth no secret understandings of any kind. The day of conquest and aggrandizement is gone by; so is also the day of secret covenants entered into in the interest of particular governments and likely at some unlooked-for moment to upset the peace of the world. It is this happy fact, now clear to the view of every public man whose thoughts do not still linger in an age that is dead and gone, which makes it possible for every nation whose purposes are consistent with justice and the peace of the world to avow nor or at any other time the objects it has in view.

"We entered this war because violations of right had occurred which touched us to the quick and made the life of our own people impossible unless they were corrected and the world secure once for all against their recurrence. What we demand in this war, therefore, is nothing peculiar to ourselves. It is that the world be made fit and safe to live in; and particularly that it be made safe for every peace-loving nation which, like our own, wishes to live its own life, determine its own institutions, be assured of justice and fair dealing by the other peoples of the world as against force and selfish aggression. All the peoples of the world are in effect partners in this interest, and for our own part we see very clearly that unless justice be done to others it will not be done to us."

—*Fourteen Points* by Woodrow Wilson.

399. Which of the following is the most accurate description of the fundamental difference behind what Woodrow Wilson expected from the treaty ending World War I and what the Allies wanted?

(A) The Allies wanted reparations from Germany; Wilson opposed them.

(B) Wilson was hampered by the need to negotiate a treaty that would pass the Senate, whereas the Allies had no political concerns.

(C) Establishment of the League of Nations was of less importance to Wilson than it was to the British and French representatives to Versailles.

(D) Wilson wanted a peace that would not lead to another war, whereas the Allies wanted revenge.

400. Which of the following terms best reflects France's attitude toward Germany after World War I?

(A) revenge
(B) forgiveness
(C) apathy
(D) fear

401. President Wilson's Fourteen Points called for all of the following EXCEPT

(A) national self-determination
(B) the creation of a league of nations
(C) decolonization in Africa
(D) a peace without reparations

402. "The Allied and Associated Governments affirm and Germany accepts, the responsibility of Germany and her allies for causing all the loss and damage . . . as a consequence of the war."

Which of the following best states one purpose of this clause from the Treaty of Versailles?

(A) to give the League of Nations the power to impose economic and military sanctions
(B) to provide a basis for international disarmament talks
(C) to include Germany in the peace negotiations
(D) to justify large reparations payments from Germany

(END OF THE WILSON QUESTION SET)

403. After World War I, Palestine, Syria, Lebanon, Jordan, and Iraq came under the control of Britain and France. These British- and French-administered territories were called

(A) demilitarized zones
(B) spheres of influence
(C) free-trade zones
(D) mandates

404. What was the name of the secret agreement by which Britain and France agreed to partition the Middle Eastern countries between them after World War I?

(A) Sykes-Picot Agreement
(B) Oslo Accords
(C) Balfour Declaration
(D) Faisal-Weizmann Agreement

405. The mandate system, created by the League of Nations, was a form
   of colonialism where the colonial rulers were

   (A) pledged to allow the inhabitants to establish self-rule
       immediately
   (B) allowed to annex all former German colonies
   (C) to appoint a provisional government immediately that was
       composed of the intellectual elites of those territories to rule
       their countries in the name of the League of Nations for a
       period of 30 years
   (D) accountable for the well-being of the inhabitants with the
       ultimate goal of teaching them how to rule themselves

406. The Balfour Declaration

   (A) was a British proposal to recognize a Jewish homeland in
       Palestine
   (B) established the border between Jordan and Israel
   (C) announced that the British would pull out of India
   (D) determined the border between India and Pakistan

407. Which state existed in 1919 but NOT in 1914?

   (A) Poland
   (B) Belgium
   (C) Croatia
   (D) Bulgaria

408. The most serious error in the Versailles Treaty that contributed to
   the breakout of the World War II was

   (A) the reversal of Brest-Litovsk
   (B) freedom for Estonia
   (C) the harsh conditions imposed on Germany
   (D) the failure to establish economic sanctions against the
       Soviet Union

409. Which of the following countries became independent as a result of
   World War I?

   (A) Portugal
   (B) Lithuania
   (C) Egypt
   (D) Austria

410. "The three national designations—Serbs, Croats, and Slovenes are equal before the law throughout the territory of the Kingdom and everyone may use them freely upon all occasions of public life and in dealing with the authorities."

This statement refers to what country?

(A) Yugoslavia
(B) Czechoslovakia
(C) Poland
(D) Bulgaria

411. Which of the following was NOT a provision of the Treaty of Versailles?

(A) Germany accepted sole responsibility for starting World War I.
(B) Austria was required to pay reparations to the Allies.
(C) Germany was effectively disarmed and the Rhineland was demilitarized.
(D) Germany was to pay the cost of damage done to the property of Allied civilians.

412. France regained which of the following as part of the peace settlement after World War I?

(A) Alsace-Lorraine
(B) Flanders
(C) the Rhineland
(D) the Ruhr

413. Which of the following countries lost the most land as a result of fighting during World War I?

(A) Germany
(B) Austria
(C) Russia
(D) the Ottoman Empire

414. Which European countries felt the impact of the Great Depression before the United States?

(A) the United Kingdom
(B) France
(C) Germany
(D) the Netherlands

415. In the 1920s and 1930s, Czechoslovakia differed from the other states in Eastern Europe by

(A) being a member of the League of Nations
(B) being a constitutional monarchy
(C) enjoying Soviet support
(D) being the only state to maintain a democratic form of government

416. Which post–World War II leader is NOT paired with the country he led?

(A) MacMillan and England
(B) Tito and Italy
(C) Khrushchev and the Soviet Union
(D) de Gaulle and France

417. The collapse of the Fourth Republic and the rise of the Fifth Republic occurred in France over

(A) fear of renewed war with Germany
(B) economic collapse
(C) a Socialist welfare policy
(D) the independence movement in Algeria

Use the excerpt below and your knowledge of history to answer the questions that follow:

The Iron Curtain

"From Stettin in the Baltic to Trieste in the Adriatic, an iron curtain has descended across the Continent. Behind that line lie all the capitals of the ancient states of Central and Eastern Europe. Warsaw, Berlin, Prague, Vienna, Budapest, Belgrade, Bucharest and Sofia; all these famous cities and the populations around them lie in what I must call the Soviet sphere, and all are subject, in one form or another, not only to Soviet influence but to a very high and in some cases increasing measure of control from Moscow."

—Excerpt from Winston Churchill's speech, March 5, 1946

418. The decision of the East German government to erect a wall dividing East Berlin and West Berlin

(A) was made in 1961 to halt the flow of refugees from East Germany

(B) prevented the infiltration of Western spies into East Berlin

(C) occurred immediately following the outbreak of the Korean War to symbolize Communist disenchantment with the West

(D) was intended to illustrate that East Germany would never again unite with West Germany

419. After the division of Germany, Berlin remained in _____ occupied territory.

(A) American

(B) British

(C) United Nations

(D) Soviet

420. Which of the following world leaders described the Cold War division of Europe as an "Iron Curtain"?

(A) Reagan

(B) Churchill

(C) Stalin

(D) Khrushchev

421. Which Communist country successfully asserted its independence from Moscow's control soon after the end of World War II?

(A) Bulgaria
(B) Poland
(C) Yugoslavia
(D) Czechoslovakia

422. The most serious post–World War II split in the worldwide Communist movement was

(A) the rupture of the Soviet-Chinese alliance
(B) the defection of Marshall Tito
(C) the Ceausescu regime in Romania
(D) the loss of Albania

423. As France's president, Charles de Gaulle's policy during the Cold War was to

(A) remain independent of both superpowers
(B) make France the leading member of NATO
(C) form a close military and economic alliance with Britain and West Germany
(D) closely align France with the Warsaw Pact nations

424. Which of the following countries is NOT a permanent member of the United Nations Security Council?

(A) the United States
(B) Germany
(C) France
(D) Russia

425. The Truman Doctrine was made in response to threats of Communist advances in

(A) China and Vietnam
(B) Greece and Turkey
(C) West Germany and Italy
(D) France and Algeria

426. The European Economic Community had its origins in an agreement about

(A) agricultural production
(B) coal and steel production
(C) railway operation
(D) river navigation

427. Which of the following countries was NOT one of the initial six members of the European Economic Community, commonly called the Common Market, following its creation in 1958?

(A) France
(B) Germany
(C) Italy
(D) United Kingdom

428. The initial accomplishments of the European Economic Community included all of the following EXCEPT

(A) Custom duties were eliminated between member countries
(B) Common policies were developed for agriculture and transportation
(C) Businesses were able to move their workforce and capital across borders
(D) Travelers from member countries could move freely across borders

429. Which statement best explains why many violent clashes have broken out between ethnic and religious groups in Central and Eastern Europe since the fall of Communism?

(A) The opening of Eastern Europe to a free-market economy has promoted ferocious competition, which has provoked ethnic hatred.
(B) Under Communism the different ethnic and religious groups were allowed complete freedom, but under the new governments they are repressed.
(C) The Eastern Europeans have simply imitated the growing nationalism in Russia.
(D) The Communist regimes suppressed or permitted only cultural expression of national ambitions, and now these ethnic differences have resurfaced.

Use the excerpt below and your knowledge of history to answer the questions that follow:

India's Fight for Freedom

"Here is a mantra, a short one, that I give to you. You may imprint it on your hearts and let every breath of yours give expression to it. The mantra is 'Do or Die.' We shall either free India or die in the attempt; we shall not live to see the perpetuation of our slavery. Every true Congressman or woman will join the struggle with inflexible determination not to remain alive to see the country in bondage and slavery."

—Gandhi, Speech to the Congress of Bombay, August 1942

430. The main methods of opposition to British rule that Mahatma Gandhi used were
   (A) terror and violence
   (B) lectures and writing
   (C) civil disobedience and nonviolence
   (D) literature that criticized Britain in guarded ways

431. During the Second World War, Indian leaders
   (A) sent and paid for thousands of troops to fight for the British Empire
   (B) disrupted the war effort by staging violent protests over Britain's continued colonial rule
   (C) agreed to help Britain because Britain offered it Dominion status in return
   (D) quit staging protests and promoted solidarity

KEY CONCEPT 4.2

The stresses of economic collapse and total war engendered internal conflicts within European states and created conflicting conceptions of the relationship between the individual and the state, as demonstrated in the ideological battle among liberal democracy, communism, and fascism.

—The College Board

---

432. The primary reason for the Bolshevik success in taking over the government in November 1917 was
    (A) the overwhelming support the Bolsheviks had from the masses of the Russian people
    (B) the collapse of workers' and soldiers' soviets, which had been the backbone of the Provisional government support
    (C) the inability of the Provisional government to solve the overwhelming problems facing the Russian people
    (D) the support given to Lenin and the Bolsheviks by Western democracies that wished to keep Russia in the war

433. Trotsky's and Stalin's interpretations of Marxism differed most significantly in which of the following ways?
    (A) Stalin wanted to foster revolution in Western Europe while Trotsky wanted to develop the Soviet Union first.
    (B) Trotsky wanted to foster world revolution while Stalin wanted "to build Socialism in one country."
    (C) Trotsky was a deviationist; Stalin followed the Communist Party line.
    (D) Stalin believed that Russia was too backward to support Communism; Trotsky believed the opposite.

434. Which slogan expresses the ideal of the Bolshevik Revolution of 1917?
    (A) Bread, Land, and Peace
    (B) Liberty, Equality, Fraternity
    (C) Russification
    (D) Lebensraum

435. At the heart of the Soviet Five-Year Plan was the idea that

(A) Soviet foreign trade would improve if customers could sign five-year contracts

(B) the Communist Party should let the state handle economic policy without interfering

(C) central party-state control could replace capitalist self-regulation of economic resources

(D) Soviet citizens should be allowed to own their own small stores and shops

436. Lenin had to adapt pure Marxist ideology to the situation in Russia because

(A) workers in Russia played virtually no part in the activities of March 1917

(B) the majority of Russians were peasants, and Marx said little about peasants' revolutionary potential

(C) Marxism had taken on too much of a religious nature, and religion did not appeal to the atheistic masses in Russia

(D) few revolutionary groups in Russia were acquainted with Marx's philosophy or plan of action

437. Which of the following best characterizes the Russian Provisional government of March–November 1917?

(A) a group of radical intellectuals committed to world revolution

(B) radical workers led by Communists

(C) military commanders who wanted to install a dictatorship

(D) middle-class and intellectual leaders who had little sympathy for workers and peasants

438. Which of the following best describes the essence of Lenin's New Economic Policy (NEP)?

(A) rapid industrialization and emphasis upon heavy industry

(B) trade with Western nations

(C) a significant resumption of private ownership

(D) a huge increase in consumer products

439. The Soviet-controlled Comintern was

(A) the name Stalin chose for the Communist Party
(B) the policy of covertly financing subversive organizations in Western Europe and the United States
(C) an organization that sought to coordinate revolutionary activities of the Communist Party abroad
(D) a branch of the Soviet military dedicated to acquiring overseas colonies for the Soviet Union

440. Which of the following was Vladimir Lenin's contribution to Marxist theory?

(A) The sole determinant of value is human labor.
(B) The proletariat inevitably becomes conscious of its revolutionary mission.
(C) A Communist revolution must be led by a party of professional revolutionaries.
(D) The operations of capitalists will inevitably bring about the destruction of the capitalist system.

441. Communists eliminated all internal and external opposition to their rule in Russia as early as which date?

(A) 1917
(B) 1918
(C) 1919
(D) 1921

442. Lenin fulfilled one part of his pledge for "Bread! Land! Peace!" by signing which treaty with the Allied Powers?

(A) Treaty of Versailles
(B) Treaty of Brest-Litovsk
(C) Treaty of Sévres
(D) Treaty of Trianon

443. The principal difference between the Bolsheviks and Mensheviks was that

(A) Bolsheviks wanted a constitutional monarchy
(B) Mensheviks felt that Russia must develop as a bourgeois capitalist state
(C) Mensheviks were led by men who were more ruthless
(D) Bolsheviks made an alliance with the Cadets

444. All of the following were major figures in the Russian Revolution EXCEPT

(A) Rasputin
(B) Lenin
(C) Czar Alexander II
(D) Alexander Kerensky

Use the excerpt below and your knowledge of history to answer the questions that follow:

"Today I am at the head of the strongest Army in the world, the most gigantic Air Force and of a proud Navy. Behind and around me stands the Party with which I became great and which has become great through me. . . . Our enemies must not deceive themselves—in the 2,000 years of German history known to us, our people have never been more united than today."

—Excerpt from Hitler's speech declaring war on the United States, December 11, 1941

445. Hitler's primary reason for invading the Soviet Union in 1941 was

(A) to block the westward expansion of Japan in Asia
(B) to knock the Soviet Union out of the war so that all of his forces could be focused against the French and the British
(C) to destroy Bolshevism and acquire lebensraum for German colonization
(D) to exterminate the Slavic population, which he believed to be a threat to German mastery of Europe

446. Which aspect of German strategy was employed during both World War I and World War II?

(A) a large-scale military push early in the war in the Balkans
(B) formation of an alliance with Japan
(C) violation of Belgium's neutrality in order to attack France
(D) respect for the rights of the United States on the sea

447. After Hitler occupied most of France, the remainder of the country became

(A) very prosperous

(B) Free France under Charles de Gaulle

(C) Republican France under Georges Clemenceau

(D) Vichy France under Marshall Henri Petain

448. Which of the following areas was conceded to Hitler at the Munich Conference of 1938?

(A) the Saarland

(B) Sudetenland

(C) Austria

(D) Poland

449. Which of the following was a major factor in German military victories from 1939 to 1940?

(A) overwhelming German technology and numerical superiority to the French and the English

(B) French insistence on continuing to fight, regardless of the cost

(C) Britain's campaign in Norway, which diverted British troops from Western Europe

(D) the German army's effective use of armor and air power in the blitzkrieg

450. A significant British invention that helped turn the tide in the Battle of Britain against Germany was

(A) radar

(B) V-2 rockets

(C) Tiger tanks

(D) sonar

451. The chief argument between Truman and Stalin at Potsdam in July 1945 was over

(A) free elections in Eastern Europe

(B) the numbers of tanks Americans and the Soviet Union could keep in Europe

(C) whether Soviet Jews would be compensated for the Holocaust

(D) whether or not the Soviet Union would join the United Nations

452. Fighting on the eastern front turned in favor of the Soviets when

(A) German forces were beaten by the Red Army in Poland

(B) Allied forces came to the aid of Soviet troops in Iran

(C) German forces were surrounded and captured at the crucial Battle of Stalingrad

(D) German forces mutinied and abandoned the siege of Leningrad

453. Nazi occupation in Western Europe differed from that in the East because

(A) people in Western countries were glad to collaborate with the Germans

(B) Nazi occupation was more extremely brutal in the East because of Nazi racial ideology

(C) the Nazis treated captured American and British soldiers more humanely in the West than in the East

(D) Jews were lumped together with Slavic peoples in the East and so escaped the worst of the Holocaust there

454. Which statement expressed a defense used by some Nazi war criminals at their trials in an attempt to justify their actions during World War II?

(A) In a war, loss of lives cannot be avoided.

(B) A person should be held personally responsible for his or her own actions.

(C) One is not accountable for one's behavior when following orders.

(D) Those who hold power have the right to exercise it in any way they see fit.

455. The political and social values of the Vichy government in France during World War II are best described as

(A) democratic, socialistic, peaceful

(B) radically fascist, antichurch, antielitist

(C) conservative-authoritarian, corporatist, Catholic

(D) republican, liberal, expansionist

456. At Yalta in February 1945, the Big Three agreed to

(A) postpone dealing with the question of what to do concerning Germany

(B) a postwar division of Germany into British, American, Soviet, and French occupation zones

(C) a two-bloc division in Europe with the West under American domination and the East under Soviet control

(D) commence the distribution of American financial aid under the Marshall Plan

457. In the 19th century, most European countries experienced virtually no migration. This changed dramatically in the 20th century when millions of people from all over the world migrated into Europe. The rise in migration patterns in that century was attributed to all of the following EXCEPT

(A) the decolonization movement

(B) the importation of large numbers of non-European soldiers and temporary workers during the World Wars

(C) the rising demand for laborers in Europe after the Second World War

(D) the new open-borders policy of many European countries

458. When Churchill said, "Never have so many owed so much to so few," *few* referred to

(A) the American soldiers at Normandy

(B) the Royal Air Force

(C) the naval commanders at the Dunkirk evacuation

(D) British soldiers who liberated concentration camps

459. France, unlike many European countries, has a long history of immigration, beginning in the 19th century when low birth rates and industrialization created a labor shortage and continuing into the 20th century when the devastation of the world wars and decolonization brought further immigration. By the end of the 20th century, France's immigration policy

(A) had helped the country to flourish economically

(B) had created a metropolitan community with no distinct cultures

(C) was universally considered a model for peaceful integration and cultural exchange of ideas

(D) had become much more restrictive, resulting in a sharp decline in the number of immigrants coming into the country

460. At the Battle of El Alamein, which of the following countries was victorious?

(A) Germany

(B) the Soviet Union

(C) Britain

(D) America

461. Which of the following countries was NOT present at the Munich Conference?

(A) England

(B) Germany

(C) France

(D) the Soviet Union

462. After the Munich Conference, which of the following leaders proclaimed "peace in our time"?

(A) Churchill
(B) Chamberlain
(C) Franklin D. Roosevelt
(D) Stalin

463. The Allied strategy of "island-hopping" involved

(A) taking over all of the Pacific Islands one by one to push Japan back
(B) taking over the larger, heavily fortified islands in order to break the backs of the Japanese
(C) taking over the smaller islands in order to break the supply lines of the Japanese
(D) using the air force to wipe out the larger islands so that Allied soldiers could "hop" their way to Japan

Use the visual aid below and your knowledge of history to answer the questions that follow:

Immigration Patterns in Europe in the 20th Century

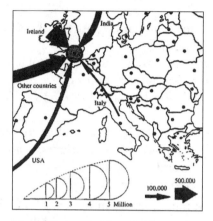

Figure 1.1   Foreign resident population in the UK, by country of origin, 1990.

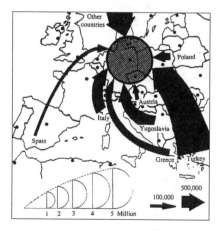

Figure 1.2   Foreign resident population in Germany, by country of origin, 1990.

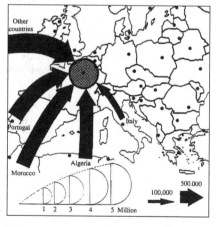

Figure 1.3   Foreign resident population in France, by country of origin, 1990.

464. Considering the migration patterns to the United Kingdom, it would be fair to say that migration to that country in the 20th century was most heavily influenced by

(A) privileged relations for residents of former colonies who were linked to the United Kingdom by common language, culture, and economies

(B) the South-North migration patterns of people seeking better economic conditions

(C) the East-West migration patterns of people seeking political asylum from communist countries

(D) the North Atlantic Treaty Organization (NATO)

465. Between 1945 and 1992, Germany took in more than 20 million displaced persons, refugees, other foreigners, and ethnic Germans from all over the world. All of the following statements about immigration to Germany are true EXCEPT

(A) German immigration was most heavily influenced by South-North migration patterns of people seeking better economic conditions.

(B) Germany was the largest European nation of immigration in the late 20th century, with more than 20 percent of its population foreign-born in the early 1990s.

(C) The reunification of Germany in 1990 had a major impact on German migration.

(D) In the decade after World War II, more than 12 million displaced persons were located in Germany.

466. After the Second World War and decolonization, immigration in France rose significantly. This was due primarily to

(A) France having a stronger economy than other European nations at that time

(B) France's location, which was so near to the countries from which the immigrants came

(C) France's immigration policy, which encouraged immigration and welcomed immigrants, especially those from its former colonies

(D) France's reputation as a destination for those seeking political asylum from communist countries

467. By the end of the 20th century, Western Europe, which had historically been a country of emigration, was

(A) facing a dwindling population and a labor shortfall

(B) trying and failing to attract immigrants to supply its workforce

(C) becoming more racially homogenous following decolonization policies

(D) having to find ways to handle mass immigration

468. Under the laws of the European Union (EU), member nations had to uphold free movement of the citizens of other member nations. This meant that member nations

(A) could not impose immigration restrictions on one another's citizens

(B) had to agree to allow a certain quota of EU immigrants into their countries

(C) had to grant all immigrants access to jobs and state welfare

(D) could not prosecute citizens from other EU countries

469. Which of the following statements is an accurate description of events?

(A) The Soviet military leadership saved millions of lives during World War II.

(B) The Maginot Line changed drastically between World War I and World War II.

(C) The Battle of Midway and the Battle of Stalingrad were similar in that both marked turning points of World War II.

(D) Military decoding work had little effect on the progress of the war.

470. Under Clement Atlee's administration, the British government

(A) undertook a major housing program

(B) strongly supported British trade unions and assumed ownership of certain major industries

(C) instituted a major program of welfare legislation

(D) all of the above

471. The Marshall Plan

(A) would supply military assistance to any country threatened by Communism

(B) excluded the Soviet Union and Eastern Europe from participation

(C) was not considered a success

(D) intended to rebuild European prosperity and stability

472. The "Prague Spring" refers to

(A) a new agricultural program introduced by the Czechoslovak Communist leadership that led to the "green revolution" in Eastern Europe

(B) the unsuccessful liberalization program attempted by Alexander Dubcek

(C) a great drought in 1968

(D) cultural flowering of Czech literature in the immediate post–World War II era

473. One of Gorbachev's key policies was perestroika, which meant

(A) significant restructuring of the centrally planned command economy

(B) political rule by a three-person directorate

(C) abolishing the KGB and introducing free political elections

(D) at first, drastic political restructuring that Gorbachev later believed could be applied to society as a whole

474. During the Khrushchev era (1956–1964) the Soviet Union

(A) retreated from some Stalinist practices

(B) enjoyed great expansion in agricultural production

(C) sought to join NATO

(D) rapidly created a consumer economy

475. Which of the following was NOT a result of the Polish and Hungarian disturbances in 1956?

(A) They demonstrated that Austrian neutrality would not be imitated in Eastern Europe.

(B) They demonstrated the limitations of independence within the Soviet bloc.

(C) They exposed the lack of military will on the part of the West to really help freedom-fighters in Eastern Europe.

(D) They brought an end to independent action in the Soviet bloc.

476. Which event, more than any other listed, caused Khrushchev to lose the support of the Soviet people?

(A) de-Stalinization

(B) the way in which the Hungarian Revolution was handled

(C) the Cuban missile crisis

(D) the Bay of Pigs invasion

477. The Brezhnev Doctrine addressed which of the following places?

(A) Communist countries in Southeast Asia

(B) NATO countries

(C) Soviet republics

(D) countries in the Soviet sphere of influence

478. One of the reasons for the Cold War, which was fought between the Soviet Union and the United States after World War II, was

(A) the refusal of the Western powers to give the Soviet Union a role in postwar Germany

(B) the religious differences of the two countries

(C) the competition between rival political and economic systems

(D) conflict over where to establish the border between Poland and Germany

479. Margaret Thatcher's popularity rose when she successfully prevented

(A) Japan from taking Taiwan

(B) Argentina from taking the Falklands

(C) China from taking Hong Kong

(D) India from taking Burma

480. Thatcherism stressed all of the following EXCEPT

    (A) nationalization of industries
    (B) destroying the power of labor unions
    (C) sharp tax cuts
    (D) reduced government spending

481. All of the following four national leaders were born or raised behind the Iron Curtain and went on to lead democratic countries following the breakup of the Soviet empire. All four served in the 21st century EXCEPT

    (A) Angela Merkel
    (B) Vaclav Havel
    (C) Lech Walesa
    (D) Dalia Grybauskaite

482. The Solidarity movement in Poland, which ultimately toppled the Communist government, was helped by what other Polish institution?

    (A) the Polish parliament
    (B) the peasantry
    (C) the army
    (D) the Catholic Church

483. Communist Yugoslavia, which emerged shortly after the end of World War II, was made up of six republics: Slovenia, Croatia, Serbia, Bosnia, Montenegro, and Macedonia. Despite their union, there was continued unrest, and nationalistic sentiments that had been fermenting for some time erupted after the fall of the Berlin Wall in 1989. In mid-1991, war broke out among these republics as a result of

    (A) Croatia applying for NATO membership
    (B) Bosnian Muslims attacking Serbs
    (C) Slovenia and Croatia declaring their independence
    (D) Croatian, Slovenian, and Bosnian forces attacking Serbia

484. Although 2.5 million Czechoslovakian citizens signed a petition asking for a referendum on the subject and polls showed that most of its citizens were not in favor of the move, in 1993 Czechoslovakia

(A) joined both the European Community and NATO
(B) split into the Czech Republic and Slovakia
(C) sided with Serbia in the ongoing Balkan war
(D) allowed local autonomy for all ethnic minorities

KEY CONCEPT 4.3

During the 20th century, diverse intellectual and cultural movements questioned the existence of objective knowledge, the ability of reason to arrive at truth, and the role of religion in determining moral standards.

—The College Board

---

485. The most innovative Soviet postwar scientific achievement was its

(A) construction of the world's largest dam on the Volga River
(B) construction of the massive gulag network
(C) design and production of high-quality fighter planes
(D) launch of the world's first unmanned space satellite

486. All of the following are reactions to the development of nuclear weapons EXCEPT

(A) fear of "mutually assured destruction" (MAD), which led to the suspension of nuclear war
(B) the proliferation of nuclear weapons
(C) the decline in the number of guerrilla wars with their dependence on traditional weapons
(D) modern war technology, which was confined to countries that can afford it, often with traumatic consequences to the national economies

487. All of the following were 20th-century artistic movements EXCEPT

(A) Bauhaus
(B) Dadaism
(C) impressionism
(D) cubism

488. The Second Vatican Council, held in Rome from 1962–1965, had a profound effect on the Catholic Church. Not only did the council examine matters of doctrine and church law, it also sparked some very visible changes in the Church, including all of the following EXCEPT

(A) saying of the Mass in the native language of the congregants

(B) allowing women to serve as priests

(C) allowing nuns to wear modern clothing

(D) encouraging priests and nuns to engage in the modern world

489. In 2015 more than 1 million people from the Middle East sought refuge in Europe. This crisis, and the fear of resulting economic and social problems, precipitated all of these actions EXCEPT

(A) the United Kingdom voting to leave the European Union (known as Brexit)

(B) the Slovakian decision to accept only Muslim refugees into its borders

(C) Bulgaria building a barbed-wire fence along its southern border

(D) the Hungarian government's adoption of an uncompromising antirefugee position

490. In some European countries, women were granted the right to vote years earlier than their U.S. counterparts. Which of the following countries was the first to give women the vote?

(A) Poland

(B) Norway

(C) Finland

(D) Denmark

491. British women suspended their suffrage campaign in 1914 when war broke out. Prior to that it had been one of Europe's most militant movements. When did British women of all ages get the vote?

(A) 1918

(B) 1920

(C) 1928

(D) 1969

492. What is the social significance of women working in factories during World War I?

(A) Due to the wartime shortage of male workers, only women could be supervisors.

(B) Women were found to be more adept than men at close detail work.

(C) Universal suffrage had been granted with the outbreak of war, and women used the vote as leverage for getting industrial jobs.

(D) The vital contribution of women to the war effort helped in their liberation from narrow social roles.

493. Changes affecting women in Western Europe since the 1950s include

(A) greater participation in the labor force

(B) the achievement of wage equality with men

(C) a reduction in life expectancy

(D) increasing family size

494. Which European country was the last to grant women the right to vote?

(A) France

(B) Italy

(C) Switzerland

(D) Portugal

495. Elizabeth II, Queen of the United Kingdom, Canada, Australia, and New Zealand, is credited with all of the following EXCEPT

(A) helping India move to independence

(B) expressing support for the Irish peace process

(C) overseeing the growth and stability of the Commonwealth

(D) serving as Britain's longest-serving monarch

496. The European Parliament issued a resolution in 2006 that called on member states to

(A) pass laws protecting homosexuals from hate speech or violence
(B) join together and pass legislation to help stem the influx of immigrants into the EU
(C) promote women in positions of leadership in their governments
(D) be more vigilant of terrorists and terroristic activities within their borders

497. Immigration to Europe was spurred by all of the following EXCEPT

(A) instability in former colonies
(B) granting of émigré status to residents of former colonies
(C) the need for workers for industry and service sectors
(D) the desire to build multicultural societies

498. Which European country embarked on a major guest worker program in the 1960s to bring much-needed workers in from Turkey, Greece, and Syria?

(A) France
(B) Sweden
(C) the Netherlands
(D) West Germany

499. Immigration was not limited to democratic countries in Europe in the 1960s. Which country under Soviet control brought in immigrant workers?

(A) Poland
(B) Hungary
(C) Czechoslovakia
(D) East Germany

500. Because human rights have gained prominence politically over the last hundred years, all of the following countries legalized homosexual acts between consenting adults in the 20th century EXCEPT

(A) Poland
(B) Germany
(C) Russia
(D) France

ANSWERS

Period 1

1. (C) For the first time since the fall of the western portion of the Roman Empire in AD 476 and the rise to prominence of the Christian Church, the leading role of this powerful institution was challenged by the Renaissance thinkers and artists. Beginning around the first half of the 14th century, these artists and thinkers emphasized individual achievement, as opposed to crediting God for their accomplishments. Many important works of art featured secular and even pagan themes, harking back to the ancient Greco-Roman civilizations for inspiration.

2. (C) The question asks to compare cities at the center of specific historically significant eras. Florence was arguably the most important center of the Italian Renaissance, producing such luminaries as Sandro Botticelli, Michelangelo, Leonardo da Vinci, Donatello, and Machiavelli. Athens was the center of classical ancient Greek achievements in art, philosophy, mathematics, and science from 508 to 322 BC. Democracy was first practiced in Athens during this time. Socrates, Plato, and Pericles were among the famous philosophers born in Athens during this time.

3. (C) Florence was not an important trade route, but it was a very important and wealthy city during the Renaissance. Options A, B, and D are all incorrect because they were important trade routes. Naples was a thriving port city; Milan was an important connecting city between northern Europe and Italy, and its wealth came from a rich agricultural industry; and Venice dominated Mediterranean commerce as an important connection between Europe, the Byzantine Empire, and the Muslim world.

4. (A) The influx of Byzantine intellectuals who escaped Constantinople after the Ottoman conquest brought with them extensive knowledge of the ancient Greeks. This is thought to have led to the revival of Greek and Roman studies and the development of Renaissance humanism and science. Option B is incorrect as Byzantine art was known primarily for its interpretation of religious doctrines. Options C and D are also incorrect. Byzantine intellectuals were not connected with particular trade routes, and it was the merchant class's patronage of art that caused art to flourish in Italy at that time.

5. (B) Cesare Borgia was the natural son of Pope Alexander VI and was a notorious plotter and, some said, a ruthless assassin in the treacherous and dangerous world of Italian city-state politics. Sforza (A) was a famous *condottiero*, mercenary soldier, who became Duke of Milan. Frederick Barbarossa (C) (his last name was Italian for "red beard") was the 12th century Holy Roman Emperor, while Option D,

Bartolomeo Colleoni, was a noted military tactician and captain general of the Republic of Venice.

6. (B) From the period of the Renaissance until Italian unification in 1861, the Italian peninsula was the battlefield of greater powers such as Spain, France, and Austria. Because of its position in the Mediterranean, Italian merchants were in a favorable position to benefit from the commercial revolution in Europe as well as growing commercial relations with the Islamic world as a result of the Crusades.

7. (C) Although the Renaissance was predicated on rediscovering the classical works of the Greeks and the Romans, humanist writers all over Europe began writing literary works and translating the Bible in the local, vernacular languages.

8. (A) People could purchase books and read them in the privacy of their houses whenever they wanted. Most pamphlets were in the vernacular language, not Latin, making B incorrect. Although national identities were fostered by writing, at the time the goal toward integration into One Europe was nonexistent.

9. (B) What distinguished the northern Renaissance from the Italian Renaissance was the emphasis on broad social reform based on Christian teachings in the north. Christian humanists believed the best way to achieve an ethical way of life was to combine the best elements of classical and Christian cultures.

10. (B) Neither country was part of the Holy Roman Empire. Poland did, however, experience more of the Renaissance influence from Italy than Russia did because of the factors listed in A, C, and D.

11. (A) While countries across Europe felt the impact of the Renaissance, some of the world's most widely read and timeless literature was produced during this period in England, including works by William Shakespeare and John Milton.

12. (D) Castiglione published a famous book in 1528 called *The Courtier* in which he described how a young man of the upper class was to become the ideal courtly gentleman, or "Renaissance man." He was expected to have a broad background in many academic subjects, and his spiritual, physical, and intellectual capabilities should be developed in school. Castiglione's concept of education was to produce refined, upper-class men of taste and sophistication—not compulsory mass education.

13. (C) Erasmus, a Dutch Christian scholar, was the Christian humanist who is considered the greatest scholar of his time. Along with editing the New Testament, he is known for his criticism of the abuses of the Catholic Church (although he always recognized the authority of the pope). Options A, B, and D are incorrect. Machiavelli, an Italian, is famous for his writing on political science. Boccaccio, another Italian, is known as a writer and poet of the time. Petrarch, also Italian, was a great writer and is often referred to as the Father of the Renaissance.

14. (C) Isabella d'Este is often described as the epitome of the cultured, talented Renaissance woman. Lucrezia Borgia (A) and Caterina Sforza (B) were members of powerful families like Isabella, and also were well-educated, but Isabella was said to outshine all her contemporaries. Sofonisba Anguissola (D) was a 16th-century native of Cremona and the daughter of a nobleman who became one of the first internationally well-known female painters.

15. (C) Catherine was an avid patron of the arts and is credited with bringing what would become classical ballet to the French court (A), also sponsoring artists and architects (B) and (C). While she brought several Italian chefs to France when she married, their impact on French cuisine is a matter of hot debate, usually along patriotic lines with Italian food scholars touting her influence and French culinary experts downplaying it.

16. (C) Jeanne d'Arc's mission was to have Charles VII crowned and to unite France under him as that was what the voices she had heard instructed her to do. Option A is incorrect. Although she did lift the siege of Orleans, that was just one step toward her goal of crowning Charles VII. Option B is incorrect. Although she was very religious, her goal remained the mission on which the voices had sent her. Option D is also incorrect—she encouraged Charles VII to march against Paris, but that was in hopes of uniting France for him.

17. (A) Sir William Cecil was Elizabeth's advisor for most of her reign. Options B, C, and D are all incorrect. Robert Dudley was a favorite of Elizabeth's and a sometime suitor, but he was not her primary advisor. Sir Francis Walsingham was the queen's secretary and was often referred to as her "spymaster." Sir Thomas Gresham the Elder was an English merchant and financier.

18. (C) During the reigns of her three sons, France was embroiled in almost constant civil wars provoked by religious conflict. Although in the early years she compromised with Huguenots and Calvinists, by the end of her reign she adopted very hard policies against them and is blamed for many of the atrocities committed against Christians in France during that time. Options A, B, and D are all incorrect. Although the peasants had grievances and there were political power struggles, neither of these were what provoked the civil wars. She was not known for economic reforms.

19. (B) The Renaissance was an artistic and cultural movement that overwhelmingly benefitted the elites in Europe. Patrons of the arts, such as the Medici from Florence, were wealthy merchant and banking families that commissioned works of art, sculptures, and buildings in large part to promote their greatness. Humanist writers found an audience only among the minority of the population that could actually read. Male merchants and nobles were the biggest benefactors of the Renaissance, while the overwhelming portion of the population, the peasants, hardly saw the benefits of formal education or cultural enrichment.

20. (B) The Ottoman attacks on the Byzantine Empire, culminating in the sacking of Constantinople and the end of the empire in 1453, resulted in Byzantine scholars moving to Italy, not the Holy Roman Empire. There was a greater cultural and intellectual affinity between Greek scholars and Italy, stemming from their common Greco-Roman past, than there was between the Greeks and the Germanic civilization in Western Europe.

21. (C) Botticelli's painting *La Primavera* (*The Spring*) features Venus celebrating the arrival of spring. Venus is associated with fertility, prosperity, and eternal youth. These are the values that were represented by the lifestyle of the Medici, the patrons of Botticelli. *The Birth of Venus* was a celebration of human desire, eroticism, physical desire, and passion once again embodied in the pagan goddess Venus.

22. (D) Leonardo da Vinci sent a résumé to the Duke of Sforza detailing his skills as a military engineer. He was hired and worked as an engineer there for seventeen years. Da Vinci was a man of many talents. He was known for his engineering skills, his inventions, and, of course, his artwork, which included the "Mona Lisa" and "The Last Supper." Options A, B, and C are all incorrect. Michelangelo was a sculptor, painter, and architect. Caravaggio and Raphael were also well-known painters, but they did not have careers as military engineers.

23. (B) From 1503 to 1513, Julius II reigned as pope in Rome and sponsored some of the world's greatest artists, including Michelangelo, who painted the Sistine Chapel ceiling, and Raphael, whose frescoes adorn the Vatican. Pope Julius also was a patron to Donato Bramante, the architect of the Vatican. Sextus IV (A) served as pope from 1471–1484 and was a patron to Botticelli. Raphael continued to work for Leo X (C) who served as pope from 1513–1521, executing a famous portrait of the pope. Michelangelo was summoned back to Rome by Pope Paul III (D), who served from 1534–1549, to paint *The Last Judgment* on the Sistine Chapel ceiling.

24. (C) The dome over the Duomo is Brunelleschi's greatest work and it continues to dominate the Florentine skyline. The Ponte Vecchio (A) is the city's oldest bridge, built in 1345 across the Arno River. The Gates of Paradise (B) are the golden doors that took artist Lorenzo Ghiberti 27 years to complete. They were unveiled in 1452. The Uffizi Palace (D) was built by the Medici in 1560 as administrative offices and now serves as a museum.

25. (A) Mannerism, also called Late Renaissance, was a style of art that used distorted poses and elongated limbs. It emerged in the 1520s and lasted until the end of the century, when the Baroque style came into vogue. Option B is incorrect as High Renaissance art was characterized by qualities of harmony and balance. Option C is incorrect as Early Renaissance style was characterized by the incorporation of realism into its artwork. Option D is incorrect because Byzantine art featured religious symbolism.

26. (B) Inspired by ancient Greek and Roman buildings, Andrea Palladio designed many structures in the Veneto region and he is considered to be one of the most influential architects in the Western world. He inspired Jefferson's design of Monticello, and other architects used his work as a model for many of the buildings seen in the United States and state capitals. Brunelleschi (A) was Florence's famed architect whose dome dominates the city skyline. Bramante (C) was chief architect in the redesign of St. Peter's in Rome. Alberti (D) designed the Church of Santa Maria Novella in Florence, another Renaissance landmark.

27. (D) This theory is named after the ancient Greek astronomer Ptolemy (90–168). It is also known as the geocentric model of the universe. Options A and B are incorrect because Socrates and Plato were philosophers. Option C is incorrect because Diocletian was a Roman Emperor.

28. (B) Copernicus revealed his heliocentric model of the universe where the sun, and not the earth, was at the center of the universe, in his book *On the Revolutions of the Celestial Spheres*, published in 1543. Options A and C are incorrect because Isaac Newton was responsible for both the theory of gravity and the development of calculus. Option D is incorrect because the periodic table of elements was developed by Russian scientist Dmitry Mendeleyev.

29. (B) In 1609, Galileo improved on earlier existing telescopes and was able to witness the changing positions of Jupiter's moons. Option A is incorrect. Although his understanding of mathematics was advanced, it wasn't a determining factor in confirming Copernicus's theory. Option C is incorrect. Galileo claimed that the heliocentric theory didn't contradict biblical writings on the world and the earth, but he also didn't use those writings to confirm Copernicus's theory. Option D is incorrect because alchemy and astronomy are completely separate fields of study.

30. (B) The discoveries made by Copernicus, Brahe, Kepler, and Galileo advanced human understanding of the universe and directly challenged the established scientific orthodoxy of the Catholic Church. The trial of Galileo in 1633 by the Roman Inquisition best exemplifies the threat the Catholic Church felt as a result of these advances. Option A can be viewed as correct but not in Europe. Catholic missionaries like Matteo Ricci brought news of many scientific advances by European scientists to China in the 17th century but not about the heliocentric theory, since the official church still rejected the theory. Option C is incorrect because there was little collaboration between the church and the "scientific community" at that time. Option D is incorrect because the Protestant Reformation was triggered by what was viewed as corruption in the church (sale of indulgences) by Martin Luther.

31. (D) Anton Lavoisier, known as the "father of modern chemistry," developed his theories in the 18th century. Medical advances included van Leeuwenhoek's observation of bacteria and microorganisms with a microscope and William Harvey's explanation of the circulatory system. Copernicus's heliocentric theory of the universe was a major advance in astronomy, while in physics, Isaac Newton discovered the laws of gravitational motion.

32. (A) William Harvey was a 17th-century English doctor. Kepler (B) was a German mathematician, while Gessner (C) was a Swiss botanist. Andreas Vesalius (D), whose Flemish name was Andries Van Wesel, wrote one of the most influential books on human anatomy, published in 1543.

33. (D) Michel de Nostredame is famous for his prophecies. He is best known for his book *Les Propheties,* a collection of poetic quatrains. He did not publish anything on classical texts (Option A), and although he did publish books on medical science (Options B and C), these were not nearly as well received or as numerous as his works of prophecies.

34. (B) The British Parliament became more powerful during that time since it had the right to levy taxes, and monarchs needed those funds to fight the war. Although the Hundred Years' War is considered to be a milestone in the development of a national consciousness, Option A is incorrect because by the end of the Hundred Years' War, England was embroiled in the War of the Roses, an internal struggle. Option C is incorrect because Parliament did not have power to govern the nation during that time, even when the king was absent. Option D is incorrect because Parliament had the power to give or deny consent to a monarch's request for funds at the close of the 13th century, before the Hundred Years' War began.

35. (C) The longbow was the most famous weapon of the Hundred Years' War. It was responsible for many of the English victories, particularly at the beginning of the war, and men of fighting age in England were encouraged to master the weapon during periods away from the battlefield. Sports were banned on the Sabbath, but longbow tournaments were allowed, making the sport popular. Options A and B were used by both sides, which is why they are incorrect. Option D is incorrect; though mace is a medieval weapon, it was more common in earlier centuries and not widely used in the war.

36. (D) One of the causes of the Wars of the Roses was nobles faulting each other for English defeats at the end of the Hundred Years' War. Option A is incorrect as the wars had nothing to do with ideology, but with dynastic succession. Also, nobles often switched sides. Option B is incorrect because the Thirty Years' War will take place in central Europe almost 100 years later. Option C is incorrect because the Wars of the Roses ended with Henry VII becoming king, not Henry VIII.

37. (B) Noble families did the bulk of the fighting in the Wars of the Roses and many people died, continuing a social breakdown that allowed many peasants to move to towns, thereby helping to end feudalism. Option A is incorrect because the eventual king was Henry VII, who was a member of the House of Lancaster.

Option C is incorrect because the Black Death had ended 110 years before this. Option D is incorrect because the private armies had made most of the trouble, and Henry VII outlawed them at the end of the wars.

38. (D) The Magna Carta was a suppression of the king's personal powers. This translated most literally to his ability to tax. After the signing of the Magna Carta, if the king wanted to impose a tax, he had to have consent from Parliament. Options A, B, and C are all incorrect. Although the charter was supposed to inhibit the king's power in all of these areas, in practice the Magna Carta did not restrain the king's power over religion, foreign policy, or civil conflicts.

39. (D) England had the only limited monarchy at the time, thanks to the Magna Carta. Options A and B are incorrect as they had absolute monarchies. Option C is incorrect because the Netherlands was a decentralized republic.

40. (A) England was Catholic during the time of the medieval Crusades. Option B is incorrect as the *Reconquista* against the Moors was considered a Crusade. Option C is incorrect because a Crusade against the heretical Albigensians took place in southern France. Option D is incorrect as there were Crusades to convert the last strongholds of paganism in Finland and northeastern Europe.

41. (C) The disunity among the Nasrid ruling house caused a leadership vacuum. Option A is incorrect since Granada was geographically challenging for would-be conquering armies given its mountainous terrain. For many years, the emirs of Granada had paid large ransoms to the Christian forces, so (B) is incorrect. Granada did lose some of its stature as a trading center (D) as Atlantic ports in Portugal and elsewhere began to eclipse the power of Granada's trading partners, including Genoa, but that was not a decisive factor in the fall of the region's Muslim leaders.

42. (B) The Inquisition served as the enforcement arm of the Catholic Church, and the Catholic Church served as the most powerful unifying force in Spain. Catholic zeal became a hallmark of "Spanishness." Option A is incorrect because the different regions of Spain were linguistically diverse. Option C is incorrect as the *Reconquista* was a very slow process and not all Spaniards hated or even remembered the Moors. Option D is incorrect because Spain did not become a part of the Hapsburg Empire until the 16th century.

43. (B) The Holy Roman Empire over time became less centralized, not more. It gradually devolved into a confederation of principalities, with more control for local princes than for the Holy Roman Emperor. All other options are incorrect because they developed strong monarchies and more centralized government apparatuses, like bureaucracies, military structures, and tax collection systems.

44. (C) The Holy Roman Empire was mostly German speaking, but other factors prevented unification. Option A is incorrect because the emperor was elected, and the electors had an interest in selecting someone they could control, or at least work with. Option B is incorrect, because over time a strong tradition of local government evolved and the princes were loath to give up any of their power. Option D is incorrect because the Holy Roman Emperor often got into conflict with the pope and others and, therefore, had his attention diverted from making the German princes more subservient.

45. (C) Italy sticks out into the Mediterranean and provides a key entry port into Europe from the south. It is also a gateway to the Mediterranean and the Holy Land and points east for pilgrims and other travelers. This allowed a certain amount of prosperity in Italy that was not always available to other parts of Europe. Option A is incorrect because the Muslims only conquered southern Italy and that was for a limited time. Option B is incorrect because Italy did not become a center of learning until the Renaissance. Option D is incorrect because Italy was indeed attacked by barbarians during the last centuries of the Roman Empire.

46. (A) The troops were mostly made up of German mercenaries and Spanish soldiers. They had defeated the French and Papal armies for Charles V, who then found himself unable to pay them. As a result, the troops mutinied, first pillaging the nearby villages and then marching on Rome in order to find money and food. The troops only withdrew from the city after receiving a hefty bribe from the Pope several months later. Charles V was deeply embarrassed by the actions of his troops but used the weakened position of the pope to exert his influence over the papacy.

47. (A) The Hapsburg dynasty ruled over the Holy Roman Empire and Austria for almost 500 years beginning in 1438. The Tudors ruled England from 1485 to 1603, the Valois ruled France from 1358 to 1589, the Hohenzollerns ruled Prussia and then the German Empire from 1701 to 1918, the Piast dynasty was the first ruling dynasty of Poland, in power from 960 to 1370.

48. (B) One of the biggest problems plaguing the various Italian territories during the era of the Renaissance was the failure to unify under a centralized authority. As a result, Italy became the battleground of larger continental powers like France and Spain. To this point, Niccolò Machiavelli in *The Prince* urged the leaders of the various Italian states to put aside their differences and unify. Failing to do so, in 1527, Rome was sacked by troops of the Holy Roman Empire who were fighting against the French for supremacy on the Italian peninsula.

49. (A) Although Europeans during the Middle Ages and early Modern era primarily identified themselves by their religious affiliation, there was little understanding of nationalism or belonging to a nation. This is a notion that gains credence in Europe in the 19th century largely as a result of the French Revolution and the wars of Napoleon. Breaking the independent power of the nobility, the ability to raise taxes and create an army, and enlisting the support of the dominant Christian Church of the domain were all essential to building the authority of a monarch in Russia, France, and Spain.

50. (A) The Ottoman Empire began its conquest of the Balkans in 1345. In 1389 the empire defeated the Serbs at Kosovo Polje, and in 1453, it took Constantinople, renamed it Istanbul, and brought to an end the Byzantine Empire.

51. (B) Around 1650 the landed aristocracy in Poland constituted about 8 percent of the country's population, the highest in Europe. This aristocracy prohibited the consolidation of the state along absolutist lines while also failing to create an effective constitutional or parliamentary government. Monarchy in Poland was elective, and upon election by the landed aristocrats, the king had to make significant concessions to them that prohibited his accumulation of power. This ultimately weakened the Polish state in relation to its absolutist neighbors, Russia, Prussia, and Austria, all of which contributed to the three partitions of Poland that totally dismembered that state by 1796.

52. (B) With the rise of Islam in the seventh century, Arab armies looked to spread their control beyond the Arabian Peninsula. The first targets of Arab Islamic expansion were Middle Eastern and north African territories of the Byzantine Empire. Starting in the 11th century, a new threat to the Byzantine Empire came in the form of various Turkic tribes. Two of the most famous were the Seljuks and the Ottomans. By 1453 the Ottoman Turks sacked Constantinople, renamed it Istanbul, and destroyed the vestiges of the Byzantine Empire.

53. (A) Although Portugal did briefly come under the Spanish crown from 1580 to 1640, it was not part of Spain under Ferdinand and Isabella. Castile, Aragon, Grenada, and Catalonia were all incorporated into a unified Spain by them.

54. (B) The Hapsburg dynasty ruled over the Holy Roman Empire and Austria for almost 500 years beginning in 1438. The Valois dynasty ruled France from 1358 to 1589. The Carolingian dynasty ruled the Frankish kingdom that would ultimately become France and Germany from 800 to 888. The Hohenzollerns ruled Prussia and then the German Empire from 1701 to 1918.

55. (A) Venice was practically the only city on the Italian peninsula that remained independent during the 16th century. Although Charles V did not possess Venice, the Venetian leadership was in an alliance with Charles against the growing Ottoman Turkish threat in the Mediterranean Sea.

56. (D) Princes, nobles, and feudal lords saw their power and independence severely curtailed when monarchs expanded their political power on a national scale. The best example of this was the 1650–1653 uprising of nobles in France, known as the rebellion of the Fronde.

57. (D) The Peace of Augsburg was a victory for Lutherans because it officially recognized their right to exist as a Christian denomination. People who lived under a prince that declared himself Lutheran had to convert to his faith or move to territories ruled by Catholic princes.

58. (A) According to modern estimates, about a third of the population was lost as a result of the Thirty Years' War in Germany. Estimates of the casualties from the wars range from 4 million to 12 million. In addition to all the deaths caused by battles, during the Thirty Years' War, soldiers carried and passed the plague to one another and to different locations in Western Europe. Also, the war and the plague precipitated famine, which added to the death toll.

59. (C) The Peace of Augsburg recognized the right of German princes to officially identify themselves as Lutherans. Subjects living in their realm also needed to accept the Lutheran faith or move to Catholic-ruled areas. This was a defeat for Charles V. He abdicated the throne shortly afterward in 1556.

60. (D) In 1640 Charles I convened Parliament for the first time in 11 years because he needed to raise money to suppress a rebellion in Scotland. The Scots rose against attempts to impose the Anglican religion there. Option A is incorrect because England was not at war with France at this time. Option B is incorrect because Charles had absolutist tendencies and was far from open to the idea of even sharing power with Parliament. Option C is incorrect. Although Puritans in England suspected him of being sympathetic to Catholicism, there is no indication that he wanted to change his faith.

61. (D) The natural enemies of the consolidation of monarchial power were members of the nobility, who lost most of their feudal independence as a result. They also despised the upstart middle-class artisans and merchants who were becoming more and more prosperous with the expansion of commercial capitalism in Western Europe. Monarchs needed money to build up strong armies and other state institutions as well as capable and educated bureaucrats for administering the realm in an efficient manner. For this they turned increasingly to the bourgeoisie. Option A is incorrect. Although serfdom in Western Europe largely comes to an end by the 16th century, there is little connection between this and the rise of national states there. Option B is incorrect because the acquisition of foreign colonies could only happen after the consolidation of national states because larger national states could summon their financial resources to undertake a policy of colonization. Option C is incorrect because exactly the opposite needed to happen for the consolidation of the national state; that is, the power of the nobility had to be subordinated to that of the monarch or at least power needed to be shared between them. In cases where the feudal nobility remained strong (Poland, Holy Roman Empire), maintaining national unity was problematic.

62. (B) Louis XIV, who believed his rule was based on the divine right of kings, never summoned the Estates General, which hadn't been brought together by a French king since 1615. Louis XIV did have the Palace of Versailles constructed, he did support the development of art and culture, and he did continue the policies of his mentor, Cardinal Mazarin.

63. (B) William of Orange ruled as stadtholder over Holland when he was invited by English parliamentarians to depose James II and assume the throne by virtue of his marriage to Mary, the Protestant daughter of James.

64. (A) Richelieu's main goal was to strengthen the power of the state, and in 17th-century France this meant strengthening the power of the king. Richelieu did so by abolishing the Huguenots' rights, given to them in the Edict of Nantes, to have their own army and fortified cities and curtailing the freedoms of the nobility. Option B is incorrect. Although a cardinal, Richelieu's main concerns were not religious or even the promotion of the Catholic Church. Option C is incorrect. Richelieu's main foreign policy goal was to roll back the power of the Catholic Hapsburgs in Austria. To that end, Richelieu aligned France with Protestant Sweden in the Thirty Years' War. Option D is incorrect because England was not a priority for Richelieu's foreign policy.

65. (C) Gustavus Adolphus intervened in the Thirty Years' War in 1630 on the side of the Protestants, turning the tide of the war in favor of the latter. Option A is incorrect because Richelieu actually provided subsidies to the Swedish king as incentive to join the conflict against the Catholic forces of the Holy Roman Empire. Option B is incorrect because he was a belligerent on the side of the Protestants, not an intermediary. Option D is incorrect because he fought against all allies of the Catholic forces of the Holy Roman Empire.

66. (C) The Time of Troubles ended in 1613 with the election of Mikhail Romanov as the new czar by the boyar council. Option A is incorrect because the Mongol occupation ended in 1480. Option B is incorrect because the split that led to the separation of the "Old Believers" from the Russian Orthodox Church happened in 1666. Option D is incorrect because the election of Mikhail Romanov had little to do with the strengthening of serfdom in Russia. This was already taking place with a series of laws that were passed beginning in the 16th century.

67. (D) The kings of France and England taxed the great landed estates of the church, prompting the famous papal bull of 1302, directly prohibiting such taxes. King Philip of France resorted to arresting the pope, who promptly died. French influence among the cardinals elected a new pope who was dominated by Philip and took up residence in Avignon, France. Option A is incorrect as widespread use of and concern about indulgences did not seem to become a problem until the early 16th century, 200 years after the Avignon papacy. Option B is incorrect because the French seemed to be concerned only with controlling the church and being able to tax it, not whatever scandals may have been going on at the time. Option C is incorrect because this had been an issue earlier in England but not in France.

68. (A) The Avignon papacy was notorious for its splendor and wealth, using new taxes and "annates," or bishop taxes. Option B is incorrect because neither the pope nor the French seemed to be struck by a new piety at the time. Option C is incorrect because the church seemed to be losing respect and influence, not gaining it during this time. Option D is incorrect as the Holy Roman Emperor seemed to be losing power and influence during the High Middle Ages and was in constant conflict with popes and others.

69. (D) After the College of Cardinals broke into rival camps and elected two popes, a church council was called at Constance to deal with the situation. They elected a third pope, who failed to get the other two to resign. The other options are incorrect as the council was concerned about all of them, and though the councils of this time made efforts to address these issues, the primary reason was to establish a unified church under one pope.

70. (C) In the end, the Conciliar Movement was a failure, and once a single pope was finally elected, he quickly moved to consolidate power for himself within the church. The reforms of the movement were forgotten until the Reformation. Options A, B, and D are incorrect because they will not take place until the Catholic Reformation.

71. (D) The Council of Trent, which took place between 1545 and 1563, was a response to the Reformation. It defined the Catholic Church's doctrine and implemented a series of self-reforms. Option A is incorrect as the Edict of Nantes granted rights to the French Calvinistic Protestants, also known as the Huguenots. Option B is incorrect as the Peace of Augsburg was a temporary settlement within the Holy Roman Empire dealing with the coexistence of Catholicism and Lutheranism. Option C is incorrect as the Pragmatic Sanction of Bourges was an agreement passed by French conciliar members who in effect created a locally controlled church in France. Parts of that agreement were later withdrawn when the French and the pope reconciled.

72. (A) After the Muslims and then the Jews were driven out of Spain, the Spanish Inquisition focused on watching any of the newly converted ex-Muslims and ex-Jews, to make sure they were not practicing their old religions on the sly. These converts were known as Moriscos and Marranos. Option B is incorrect as these were Protestants who will not exist until later and they were also in different countries. Option C is incorrect as Jews and Muslims had already been expelled. Option D is incorrect as followers of Jan Hus were in Bohemia.

73. (B) As Ferdinand of Aragon and Isabella of Castile led the *Reconquista* of Spain from the Muslims, they received permission from the pope to hold an Inquisition against Jews and Muslims. Both groups were pressured to convert to Catholicism, forced into exile if they refused, or in some cases, killed.

74. (C) The sale of indulgences by the Catholic Church triggered the Protestant Reformation. The Council of Trent was convened to address the doctrines that the Protestants had challenged, including the issuing of indulgences. On this issue, the council did condemn "all base gain for securing indulgences," but the theory and correct practice of indulgences was reaffirmed.

75. (A) Fleeing the religious turmoil and anti-Protestant mood in France, the country of his birth, Calvin settled in Geneva in 1536.

76. (C) The selling of indulgences prompted Martin Luther to write his famous Ninety-Five Theses, which condemned the practice of selling indulgences and other papal abuses.

77. (B) In 1517 Luther issued his Ninety-Five Theses, condemning papal abuses and the selling of indulgences. In 1520, three of his best-known and most influential works were published: On the Freedom of a Christian, To the Christian Nobility of the German Nation, and On the Babylonian Captivity of the Church. In 1521 Luther was excommunicated by Pope Leo X. That same year, at the Diet of Worms, Luther refused to recant his writings in the Ninety-Five Theses. As a result, he was condemned by Emperor Charles V and subsequently given sanctuary in a castle at Wartburg by Frederick III, elector of Saxony.

78. (A) John Knox is one of the great reformers of Scotland. He was exiled for many years because of his teaching but was able to return shortly before the Reformed Protestant church was ratified by law in Scotland. After his return to Scotland, he wrote *The History of the Reformation of Scotland*, as well as other treatises. Options B, C, and D are incorrect as Luther, Savonarola, and Hus were all excommunicated because of their teaching.

79. (C) Henry VIII was not a supporter of Luther or any of the Protestant reformers. Henry's decision to break with the Catholic Church was in reaction to Pope Clement VII's refusal to grant Henry an annulment from his marriage to Catherine of Aragon, the aunt of Holy Roman Emperor Charles V.

80. (A) It was not Martin Luther's intention to break away from the Catholic Church. By issuing his Ninety-Five Theses, he appealed to Pope Leo X to correct the abuse of indulgences. Facing growing opposition from the papacy and as a result of his excommunication from the Catholic Church, Luther decided a break was necessary. Henry VIII was actually named "Defender of the Faith" by Pope Leo X for his criticism of Martin Luther. Henry broke with Rome when the pope failed to issue him an annulment to his marriage to Catherine of Aragon.

81. (B) If the power of the Ottoman Empire threatened anybody in the Christian world, it was the Orthodox Church. Eastern Orthodoxy was the main faith of the people of the Balkans, who were conquered by the Turks by the 15th century. The authority of the Catholic Church in Western Europe was challenged by the values promoted during the Renaissance, the scientific discoveries of the Scientific Revolution, and the growing authority of monarchs and their consolidation of nation-states.

82. (B) In 1559 Elizabeth and the Parliament reestablished the independence of the Church of England through two acts: the Act of Supremacy and the Act of Uniformity.

83. (A) France, a staunchly Catholic country, was surrounded by Hapsburg possessions: to the east in the Holy Roman Empire, to the north—the Netherlands, and to the south—Spain. It was in France's foreign policy interests to fan religious discord in the Holy Roman Empire, even if that meant supporting the Protestants.

84. (D) One of the biggest doctrinal differences between Luther and Calvin was the issue of predestination. Calvin held a pessimistic view of human nature and believed God knew in advance who was eligible for salvation. No amount of good earthly deeds could alter the outcome.

85. (D) Erasmus and Luther were contemporaries and for a time, friends. Erasmus, as a preeminent humanist, was highly critical of the Catholic clerical hierarchy. One of his most famous works, In Praise of Folly, published eight years before Luther's Ninety-Five Theses, criticized the corruption and superstition of the Catholic Church hierarchy. Erasmus, however, did not approve of Luther's break with the Catholic Church.

86. (C) This quote is from Luther's Ninety-Five Theses, condemning the sale of indulgences to finance the construction of St. Peter's Basilica in Rome.

87. (A) The Peace of Augsburg of 1555 recognized the right of German princes in the Holy Roman Empire to openly declare themselves either Catholic or Lutheran but not Calvinist. This was a major victory for the Lutheran movement.

88. (C) In the 1550s John Knox brought Calvinism to Scotland, where Presbyterianism became the dominant Christian denomination. Other European countries with significant Calvinist appeal were the Netherlands, Switzerland, and France (Huguenots).

89. (D) In the first Act of Supremacy of 1534, the English Parliament declared Henry VIII the only leader of the Church of England.

90. (A) It was a central tenet of Martin Luther's teachings that Christians should live by the teachings of the Bible, not the pope. In this case Luther rejects the practice of fasting because there is no basis for it in the Bible.

91. (C) Luther rejected five of the seven sacraments. The two he approved were sacramental baptism and communion. Later other Protestants would dispute Luther's interpretation of these two sacraments, causing further splits in the Protestant movement.

92. (C) King Henry IV of France issued the edict in 1598 granting religious tolerance to the Protestant Huguenots. Although the edict was not popular with Catholics and it was later renounced by Louis XIV, it did contribute to defusing the tensions that led to the religious wars in France in the 16th century.

93. (B) Many Huguenots fled France for England, Holland, Sweden, Switzerland, Prussia, Denmark, South Africa, and North America after Louis XIV's revocation of the Edict of Nantes in 1685. Option A is incorrect because it was very difficult for the Huguenots to launch an armed rebellion against Louis XIV since Cardinal Richelieu had revoked their military privileges earlier that century. Most Huguenots left France. Eventually, the Huguenots were allowed to practice their faith openly in France. Option C is incorrect as the Huguenots chose to move to other countries more favorable to Protestant beliefs. Option D is incorrect. Although the St. Bartholomew's Day massacre was directed against the Huguenots by the Catholics, it took place in 1572 and not as a result of the revocation of the Edict of Nantes.

94. (C) James II ignored the Test Act and appointed Catholics to positions of authority in the kingdom. He was openly sympathetic to Catholicism. In 1688 his Catholic wife gave birth to a son, which opened the way for a Catholic dynasty in England to emerge. Option A is incorrect; James II had good relations with France, fleeing to that country after he was deposed in 1689. Option B is incorrect because this is what ultimately happened with the support of English Protestants. Option D is incorrect because James already held the crown of both England and Ireland (as well as Scotland).

95. (A) The struggle for retaining the feudal liberties against the centralizing tendencies of monarchs defined the political struggles emerging in Europe in the 16th–18th centuries. After 1648, as a result of the Thirty Years' War and the Treaty of Westphalia, the Holy Roman Empire nominally remained intact but political power was significantly devolved to the more than 300 princes and free cities that comprised the empire. In France, this struggle resulted in the consolidation of power in the hands of powerful monarchs like Louis XIV.

96. (D) Scholars of economic history credit a light-handed regulatory approach with enabling the growth of the great trade centers as the global economy began to emerge in the 16th century.

97. (D) With their access to open Atlantic waters and the new trade routes, plus a relatively light-handed approach to regulation and an entrepreneurial atmosphere, English and Dutch ports became great centers of trade in the Age of Discovery.

98. (D) Henry the Navigator was a royal prince of Portugal who nurtured his country's maritime sector and sponsored voyages of exploration in the 15th century. His initial goal was to reach Cathay, as China was known, but he also set the stage for Portugal to reach India and other parts of Asia. He is alleged to have built a navigation school at Sagres in Portugal, which some scholars dispute; however, there is little argument over his impact on the world of global exploration since he nurtured the explorers and the scientists who developed new navigational tools.

99. (C) Vasco de Gama made three very important voyages to India, including one in 1497. Vespucci (A) explored the area around modern-day Rio de Janeiro, Brazil, on his 1501 voyage, his third to the region. In 1499 a German mapmaker named the "New World" America in Vespucci's honor. A famous Englishman, Sir Francis Drake (B) circumnavigated the globe in 1577–80, landing along the way in northern California, and possibly Oregon. Ferdinand Magellan (C) attempted to circumnavigate the globe in 1519, passing through what was to become the Straits of Magellan, off the tip of South America, in 1520. He was killed in a battle in the Philippines in 1520, but his men completed the circumnavigation.

100. (A) The Spanish clearly looked at Columbus's ideas as a way to leapfrog the Portuguese, who were having success getting to the Indian Ocean by sailing around Africa. It looked for a time that the Portuguese were about to become the masters of the seas and dominate trade to Asia. Option B is incorrect because the Spanish did not know of the existence of America yet. Option C is incorrect because it was commonly known at the time that the world was round, and the clergy had no interest in proving it otherwise. Option D is incorrect because the English had expressed no such desire yet.

101. (C) The Spanish colonies, once they were established, had extractive economies, meaning silver, gold, and other raw materials were extracted for export and sale to others outside the empire. Option A is incorrect as Spanish America was known for the same religious intolerance that characterized Spain at the time. Option B is incorrect because the colonies were tightly controlled by Spain. Option D is incorrect because the Spanish tried to superimpose Spanish culture onto the natives.

102. (D) The encomienda system was a way for Spain to abuse native labor on estates in the New World. It bore a striking resemblance to European feudalism in that the natives had some rights and were only required to work for the landowner two days a week, reserving the other four workdays for their own land. All other options are incorrect because they refer to noneconomic institutions.

103. **(A)** The descendants of the original Spanish settlers were called Creoles. Option B is incorrect as peninsulares were Spaniards in America who had actually come from Spain. They were at the top of the social structure but were the smallest in number. Options C and D refer to the children of Africans and Spanish, and Indians and Spanish, respectively.

104. **(A)** The purpose of the Treaty of Tordesillas was to divide the world between the two Catholic colonial powers: Spain and Portugal. It renegotiated the imaginary line of demarcation set by Pope Alexander VI in 1493 that ran north-south in the middle of the Atlantic Ocean. The treaty granted Spain most of South America (except Brazil) and points west (eventually including the Philippines) while Portugal was granted Africa and Asia (points east of the line of demarcation).

105. **(C)** Bartolome de las Casas wrote *A Short Account of the Destruction of the Indies* in 1542 (published in 1552) and sent it to Prince Philip II of Spain to inform him of the cruel treatment of Native Americans by the Spanish colonial authorities. The book was not written with the intent to destabilize the Spanish monarchy politically or criticize Catholic doctrine or practice, nor was it written for personal gain.

106. **(B)** The Crusades were launched in 1095 by Pope Urban II to ostensibly help the Byzantine emperor Alexis regain control of Jerusalem, which had fallen under Muslim rule since the seventh century. The First Crusade (1095–1099) was a military success for the Christian Crusaders, resulting in colonies being established in the Levant. Although ultimately the Muslims defeated the Christian Crusaders and these colonies were abandoned, other than the Vikings' invasion of Greenland, it was the first time since Roman times that Western Europeans had ventured beyond their boundaries in a concerted effort to colonize non-European territory.

107. **(D)** Japan at this time (16th century) largely isolated itself to the outside world of trade and foreign cultural contacts. The only European people that made any headway with the Japanese at this time were the Dutch, not the Portuguese. Japan was also not a prized destination for goods at this time. More sought after were the goods from China, the Spice Islands (Indonesia), and India.

108. **(A)** The high price of goods coming from the East was one of the most important reasons why the Portuguese and Spaniards looked for alternatives to the traditional overland trade routes between Europe and the Far East. By the end of the 16th century and the fall of the Mongol Empire, the Silk Road was no longer a viable and safe trade route. The Portuguese had begun using the Indian Ocean more to get to India and the Spice Islands while the Spaniards sailed west across the Atlantic hoping to reach the Spice Islands and India in the East.

109. (D) There was no "Germany" during the Age of Exploration. Germanic people and territories were part of the Holy Roman Empire during this time. Germany would not become an independent country until 1871.

110. (A) Along with mastering navigational technology, the Spanish and Portuguese also used military means to achieve their early domination of overseas exploration and colonization. The Portuguese militarily forced the Arabs out of the lucrative Indian Ocean trade while the Spaniards, with superior arms, were able to subjugate most of Latin America with a numerically inferior fighting force in comparison to the natives they encountered.

111. (B) Sugarcane production and harvesting is very labor intensive, requiring many peasants to work on plantations. The demand for sugar increased greatly from the 16th century as global commercial connections increased and goods such as coffee, tea, and chocolate became more popular. Sugar became an important cash crop for colonial European powers such as Spain, France, and England.

112. (C) The Columbian Exchange, named after Christopher Columbus, is the result of the contacts established between European explorers, colonists, merchants, and Native Americans in the Western Hemisphere and Africans. The significance of the Columbian Exchange is that it initiates the first truly global epoch of world history and signifies the growing importance of Europe and its eventual world dominance.

113. (A) Because of a shift in the climate at the beginning of the 14th century, harvests began to fall short during this time, leading to famines. Some historians believe that when the Black Death arrived, it affected an already weakened population in Europe. Option B is incorrect as the Renaissance is considered to have begun during the latter part of the 14th century at the earliest. Option C is incorrect as conflict was common in the 14th century, particularly since the Hundred Years' War had begun just 10 years earlier. Option (D) is incorrect as most historians date the beginning of the Reformation to the early 1500s.

114. (C) Fleas and the bacteria that they carry are the actual reason for the Black Death. Europeans at the time had no idea of the actual cause. Option A is incorrect because Jews were rumored to have poisoned wells and whole Jewish communities were destroyed. Option B is incorrect, as many believed that sin warranted self-flagellation, which would show repentance and perhaps move God to intervene. Option D is incorrect because many believed that breathing bad air could cause disease and fled to the country.

115. (A) Because of the reduced numbers of laborers, the Black Death had the effect of raising the wages of those who survived. Option B is incorrect as it is exactly the opposite of the correct option. Option C is incorrect because the economic disruptions of the Black Death destabilized feudalism and created social mobility in the general breakdown of order and custom. Option D is incorrect because the Hundred Years' War ended 90 years after the Black Death.

116. (D) Except in the highly urbanized areas of northern Italy and Flanders, peasants constituted 85 to 90 percent of the total European population.

117. (D) Sixteenth-century Western European families were predominantly nuclear composed of a married couple and their children. Farther east, in Hungary and Muscovite Russia, taxation favored households that did encourage extended families. There several nuclear families often lived in the same household.

118. (D) The Medici family, particularly under Cosimo (1389–1464) and Lorenzo (1449–1492), were patrons to some of the most important Renaissance figures of the time: Filippo Brunelleschi, Donatello, Botticelli, Michelangelo, and Leonardo da Vinci.

119. (D) Europe in the early Modern era consisted of three basic classes or estates: the clergy, the nobility, and the peasants. The royal families that were emerging in various European states were not considered a separate estate or class. The bourgeoisie, although rising in economic significance since the commercial revolution beginning in the 13th century, were still insignificant politically and not a separate estate. Finally, there was no proletariat until the Industrial Revolution in England in the 18th–19th centuries.

120. (C) France's population in 1600 was approximately 20 million. In comparison, Spain's population was about 8 million, Russia's was 13 to 15 million, England's was 4.4 million, and Poland's was 8 to 10 million.

121. (A) Men of the middle class were typically not army officers. High-ranking positions in the military during this period of time were most often reserved for the nobility. Options B, C, and D are incorrect as people from the middle class often pursued professions such as lawyers, bankers, and shopkeepers. This was especially true after the rise of trade in Europe, which resulted in the commercial revolution.

122. (D) Inspired by Luther's challenge to the Catholic Church, German peasants seized the opportunity to revolt against their oppressive social and economic conditions. Luther harshly condemned their rebellion and urged the secular authorities to ruthlessly crush the uprising.

Period 2

123. (C) Enlightened despots curbed the power of the church, but they did not "abolish" any religions. The other options are reforms implemented by Joseph II of Austria, Frederick the Great of Prussia, and Catherine the Great of Russia.

124. (B) Constitutional rule was not acceptable to absolutist rulers. All other options are essential characteristics of absolutist states.

125. (A) In 17th-century Europe, the justification of political authority largely rested on the theory of divine right of kings, whereby the king was the political embodiment of God's ultimate representative on earth. As such, his power was absolute and not to be challenged by any persons or institutions, like a parliament. Option B is incorrect because since the Protestant Reformation and the rise of the nation-state, papal power declined while secular power increased. Whereas in the Middle Ages, papal authority could claim to be God's representative on earth, this began to change with the rise of absolute monarchy. Option C is incorrect as the rights of subjects were to become an issue during the Enlightenment, beginning in the 18th century. Option D is incorrect because, although the papacy would have liked to have this type of power over secular authority, with the rise of absolutism, spiritual power took a back seat to secular authority.

126. (C) Option A is incorrect as Charles I was the king of England that Cromwell's supporters fought in the civil war. Option D is incorrect because John Pym was a leader of the Long Parliament and a prominent opponent of Charles I, but he wasn't the leader of the Roundheads.

127. (A) Tensions between Parliament and Charles I began in 1628 when Parliament forced Charles to agree to the Petition of Right, which stipulated that he must gain the consent of Parliament before he could raise new taxes. In response, Charles refused to call Parliament into session between 1629 and 1640. When Charles tried to bring Anglican reforms to Presbyterian Scotland, the Scots revolted. To raise money to fight the war, Charles called Parliament into session, which then brought the conflict between the monarch and Parliament to a head.

128. (C) Prior to the outbreak of the English Civil War, Charles attempted to raise taxes without the consent of Parliament. This attempt was to raise "ship money." This tax was intended to finance a modern navy by taxing everyone, not just residents of coastal towns. In 1640 Charles reluctantly convened Parliament because he needed money to put down a rebellion in Scotland. The Parliament used the Scottish rebellion to press its demands against Charles.

129. (A) Captured by Oliver Cromwell's forces while trying to flee to Scotland, Charles I was tried by a much smaller Parliament of about 53 members, convicted of treason, and sentenced to death by beheading. Option B is incorrect because the Tudor line ended with the death of Queen Elizabeth in 1603. James VI of Scotland assumed the English throne unopposed. In Option C, the execution of Charles I did lead to the abolition of the monarchy and the establishment of a republic (the English Commonwealth). But the republic was short-lived; it ended with Cromwell's death, and the military reestablished the monarchy by inviting back Charles I's eldest son. Option D did not occur as a result of Charles's execution, as Cromwell's forces crushed any remnants of opposition from those two nations.

130. (D) After executing Charles I in 1649, Oliver Cromwell declared England to be a republic and named the country the Commonwealth. But his domestic policies led to growing opposition to his republic, and he disbanded the Rump Parliament in 1653, naming himself "Lord Protector." Option A is incorrect because all forms of monarchy were abolished by the "Rump Parliament" and the Council of State shortly after the execution of Charles I. Although Cromwell was a strict Puritan who saw himself as "God's agent," his rule cannot be considered a theocracy, rendering Option B incorrect. Option C is incorrect as Cromwell's republic may have begun as something resembling a parliamentary republic, but by 1653, he abolished this institution when opposition to his domestic economic policies grew.

131. (B) Although Cromwell did enter into a secret alliance with France against Spain, it cannot be said that his government relied on France for its survival. Landowners and merchants in the Rump Parliament did increasingly oppose Cromwell's taxation policies that were intended to fund his wars against the Spaniards. This led to its disbanding in 1653. In Option A, the majority of England's population did reject the more extreme Puritan-inspired policies of Cromwell's government, like the ban on sports, theaters, and pubs, and the transformation of feast days in honor of saints to fast days, among other things. In Option C, Cromwell's brutal military campaign in Ireland (1649–1650) that led to the occupation of that country by British forces resulted in him being one of the most hated figures in Irish history. In Option D, Cromwell alienated many republicans and religious radicals by dissolving the Rump Parliament and taking on the title of "Lord Protector" for life.

132. (D) After an initial "honeymoon" period of mutual understanding between Charles II and the Parliament, relations began to deteriorate when Charles exhibited his admiration for French King Louis XIV and openly declared his support for the principle of religious toleration. Parliament interpreted this as his way of promoting Catholicism in England. Parliament also feared the ascension to power of his younger brother and heir James, who had publicly announced his conversion to Catholicism in 1668.

133. (C) The English Civil War had been largely triggered by the struggle between the Stuart monarchs who favored royal absolutism and Parliament, which favored a power-sharing arrangement between itself and the king. In 1688 and 1689 the conflict had been resolved when James II abdicated and William of Orange and Mary accepted the throne from Parliament on agreement that they would share power. Option A is incorrect as this took place in 1707 in the Act of Union by the Parliaments of England and Scotland. Option B is incorrect because if this would have happened, the anti-British uprising in the American colonies may not have taken place. Option D is incorrect because the Industrial Revolution, beginning around 1750, contributed more than any other single factor to England's rise to supremacy in Europe. After the unification of Germany in 1871, England's dominant position in Europe was significantly challenged.

134. (C) The English Bill of Rights of 1689 set the limits of monarchial power as well as defined the rights of Parliament. Option A is incorrect because the Levellers were a political movement during the civil war that demanded constitutional reform and equal rights under the law. The Leveller movement was ended by the forces of Cromwell in 1649. Option B is incorrect as the Magna Carta dates to 1215. Option D is incorrect because the Long Parliament was convened by Charles I in 1640 to raise money for an army to suppress a rebellion in Scotland.

135. (D) The events in England of 1688 were known as the Glorious Revolution because English constitutionalism and parliamentary government triumphed over an overbearing monarchy. At the same time, after 1688, membership in Parliament became more exclusive: an act of 1710 required members of the House of Commons to possess private incomes at such a level that only a few thousand people could legally qualify. This income had to come from ownership of land, indicating the aristocratic and oligarchic nature of British government during this period.

136. (B) These discriminatory policies targeted Ireland for fear that Ireland would foment a pro-Catholic uprising against the English and to prevent it from entering any potentially anti-English alliances. Option A is incorrect as England and Scotland would soon sign the Act of Union in 1707, joining the two countries in the United Kingdom. Option C is incorrect as England would not have the right to impose these policies on sovereign states. Option D is incorrect as there were hardly any Catholics in Wales.

137. (B) In 1701 the Act of Settlement stipulated that no Catholic could be king of England in response to the pro-Catholic sentiments of James II, who was deposed in 1688 by the English Parliament, and William of Orange, chosen to replace James. Option A is incorrect as the Solemn League and Covenant, passed by Parliament during the English Civil War in 1642, called for Presbyterianism to be the united faith of England, Scotland, and Ireland. Parliament passed the act to gain the support of the Scots against pro-Charles I Royalist forces. Option C is incorrect as the Petition of Right of 1628 called for Charles I to honor four specific constitutional principles: no taxation without Parliament's consent; no imprisonment without just cause; no forced billeting of soldiers; and no martial law in time of peace. Option D is incorrect as the English Bill of Rights, enacted in 1689, confirmed the principle of power-sharing between the English monarch and the Parliament. The king could not raise taxes or an army without the consent of Parliament, and no subject could be arrested and detained without due process. William III (Orange) had to accept these principles prior to the throne being offered to him.

138. (D) The landed aristocracy prohibited the consolidation of the state along absolutist lines as well as the creation of an effective constitutional or parliamentary government. As in the Holy Roman Empire, Polish kings were elected at a time when some of the country's neighbors, namely Austria, Prussia, and Russia, were consolidating their states along solidly absolutist principles. Option A is incorrect because serfdom, far from being abolished, was strengthened in Poland during the 18th century. Option B is incorrect because Sweden was no longer a European military power after Charles XII died in battle in Norway in 1718. Option C is incorrect because Poland's real threats came from Russia, Austria, and Prussia.

139. (A) All three countries bordered Russia in the west/northwest (Poland, Sweden) and south (Ottoman Empire), and all were considered to be European powers. Option B is incorrect as Holland, England, and the Holy Roman Empire were too preoccupied with other more important conflicts (English Civil War, the Thirty Years' War). Option C is incorrect mainly because Hungary was not an independent state at this time. It was divided between the Ottoman Turks and Austrian Hapsburgs. Option D is incorrect because England and France were preoccupied with other conflicts.

140. (D) Ukraine and its capital city, Kiev, was the capital of the first Russian state (Kievan Rus'). From the mid-14th century until 1653, Ukraine was under the rule of the Polish-Lithuanian state. Option A is incorrect because Belarus shared a similar fate to that of Ukraine; that is, it was contested by Poland-Lithuania and Russia. Option B is incorrect since Latvia was not an independent state until 1918. Option C is incorrect because Estonia was not an independent state until 1918, and Sweden never extended its control into Ukraine.

141. (C) At the onset of the Haitian Revolution, black slaves made up at least 90 percent of the population of the country. The Haitian Revolution, which lasted from 1791 to 1804, was an important event in world history. It was a struggle for equal rights for all men, regardless of color, and was one of the first times that the principles of individual freedoms declared in the American and French revolutions were applied to people of color. It was also the only successful slave revolt in human history and resulted in the declaration of Haiti as a free state.

142. (B) The mulattoes, or "yellows," were the driving force behind the Haitian fight for freedom. Mulattoes were considered freemen but did not have the same civil rights as white people in Haiti. After the outbreak of the French Revolution, the mulattoes in Haiti began demanding equal rights. They were granted citizenship by Paris in 1791, but the white population in Haiti tried to refuse to do the same. Option A is incorrect as the slaves did not revolt until 1792. Option C is incorrect because maroons had formed their own communities and signed peace treaties that granted them freedom in the mid–18th century, well before the Haitian Revolution. Option D is also incorrect as the European colonists were happy with the status quo at the time.

143. (B) After the revolution, many European countries treated Haiti with open hostility. This was because the Haitian Revolution went against their ideology, and they could not conceive of establishing trade relations with a black nation. Option A is incorrect because the United States, despite its fears, continued to trade with Haiti after the revolution. Option C is incorrect because the demand for sugar did not decrease. Cuba stepped in as the foremost producer of sugar after the Haitian Revolution. Option D is also incorrect. Although there continued to be unrest within its own borders, Haiti was not at war with its neighbors.

144. (B) As an enlightened despot, Joseph II believed that far-reaching reforms were the responsibility of the monarch and the state. Enlightened despots were not to be subjected to elections. All other options are reforms of Joseph II.

145. (D) One of Maria Theresa's main goals while in power was to prevent the dissolution of the monarchy. To that end, her administration broke the control of territorial nobles in their diets. The Bohemian and Austrian provinces were welded together (the kingdom of Bohemia losing its constitutional charter in 1749). Under Joseph II, regional diets and aristocratic self-government fared even worse. Unlike his mother, Joseph also applied his centralizing policies in Hungary. He made German the official administrative language in a country made up of Poles, Czechs, Magyars, Slovenes, and others.

146. (A) With the "Germanization" of the Slavic and Magyar population of the Austrian Empire, nationalism among the Czechs, Poles, and Hungarians grew to become a threat to the empire in the next century. Option B is incorrect because both Prussia and Austria increasingly saw themselves as the leaders of the German world in Europe. Talk of unification would have been antithetical to their desire to be the leaders. Option C is incorrect. Although it was during Joseph II's rule that the first partition of Poland, with Austria's participation, took place, this had nothing to do with Joseph's "Germanization" policy. Option D is incorrect because making the German language the main administrative language of the Austrian Empire was not opposed by the German-speaking Prussians.

147. (B) The Junkers were the commanders of the Prussian army and, therefore, could not be antagonized by reforms that would break their hold on their serfs. This is the reason why Option A is incorrect. Option C is incorrect because the number of serfs on crown lands was only about 25 percent of all serfs. Option D is incorrect because although Frederick was an enlightened despot and did move to alleviate serfdom, moral considerations had less to do with abolishing it on crown lands than appeasing the Junkers.

148. (A) Frederick was anything but a mediocre leader with limited intelligence and ambition. His talents and intelligence were recognized by no less of a luminary than Voltaire. All other options accurately describe Frederick's rule.

149. (A) The Pugachev Rebellion, a peasant rebellion led by Emelian Pugachev, had to be suppressed violently by the Russian army under Catherine in 1774. It was the largest peasant revolt in European history and it shook Catherine. Less than 20 years later, the French Revolution broke out. Both of these revolts led to Catherine curtailing her reforms and becoming more politically conservative. Option B is incorrect as the wars against the Ottoman Turks and the partitions of Poland led to the strengthening and expansion of the Russian state but had little effect on reforms. Options C and D are incorrect because neither Catherine's social life nor the American Revolution had an impact on her reform efforts.

150. (B) Russian forces under Catherine defeated the Turks twice and took full control of the Crimean Peninsula by 1792. Russia also benefited from the three partitions of Poland, expanding its borders westward. Option A is incorrect because Russia's expansion into Central Asia took place in the 19th century. Option C is incorrect because there was no such attempt on the part of Russia to enter into an alliance with China. Option D is incorrect because it was Peter the Great who defeated the Swedes in the Great Northern War.

151. (C) Joseph II of Austria went further than any other European monarch up to the French Revolution in granting equal civil rights to Jews. He allowed Jews to obtain noble status, but with that he also made them equal in service to the king, which meant they had to serve in the military. Options A and D are incorrect because neither ruler was known to be an enlightened despot. Louis XVI's failure to enact any substantial reforms contributed to the outbreak of revolution in France in 1789, while Philip II (1527–1598) was an extremely conservative Catholic ruler of Spain who intensified the work of the Inquisition. As to Option B Frederick the Great did not implement any reforms that specifically dealt with the Jews.

152. (B) In response to the largest peasant rebellion in European history, Catherine strengthened and expanded serfdom into the Ukrainian territories of the Russian Empire. Option A is incorrect because the opposite occurred. Options C and D never occurred.

153. (A) Ultimately, enlightened despots needed the support of the nobility, which they never fully received because the monarchs looked to further undercut the nobles' power. Once the enlightened despots were gone in Russia and Prussia, for example, the power of the nobles, at least over their serfs, returned. Option B is incorrect because while enlightened despotism may have introduced the concept that reform comes from the state, no provisions were made to create a welfare state and enlightened despots were thoroughly opposed to any sort of democratic limitations to their power. Option C is incorrect because the attempt to return to absolute rule was more in response to the upheavals resulting from the French Revolution than to the changes brought by enlightened despotism. Option D is incorrect because the opposite occurred. Political power was more centralized as a result of enlightened despotism.

154. (A) Louis considered religious unity necessary to the strength of France and his royal authority. To that end, in 1685 Louis revoked the Edict of Nantes. As a result, many Huguenots left France for Holland, Germany, and America. Option B is incorrect because the First and Second Estates continued to enjoy tax-free status until the French Revolution. Option C is incorrect because as an absolute ruler, Louis was not interested in the Estates General or any other institution limiting his power. The first part of Option D is generally correct but the second part—the monarch answering to the pope—is incorrect. Once again, as absolute monarch, Louis was convinced of his absolute authority to rule given to him by the good graces of God and not a temporal authority even in the form of the leader of the Catholic Church.

155. (A) In 1685 Louis XIV revoked the Edict of Nantes, which was issued by Henry IV in 1598 as a means to end the religious wars that engulfed France in the 16th century. The edict provided the right to Huguenots to practice their brand of Christianity in the towns where they predominated and to extend them the same rights as Catholics. Option B is incorrect because the Ninety-Five Theses was Martin Luther's list of grievances against abuses of the Catholic pope. In Option C, the Edict of Fontainebleau is the revocation of the Edict of Nantes. It is the wrong option because the question states: this statement was most likely issued as a result of the Edict of Nantes. Option D is incorrect because the Peace of Augsburg of 1555 put an end to the war between an alliance of Lutheran princes and free German cities known as the League of Shmalkald and the Catholic forces of Holy Roman Emperor Charles V. Incidentally, the Peace of Augsburg was a victory for Protestants, as it recognized for the first time the right of each state and free city within the empire to choose Catholicism or Lutheranism as its faith.

156. (D) Louis XV presided over the decline of royal absolutism in France. Wars and excesses drained the treasury during his reign, and he often left the affairs of state to his ministers while he engaged in hunting and womanizing. The result was a disillusionment of the citizenry with the monarchy in general. Henry IV (Option A) is inaccurate as Henry IV can be seen as the monarch who laid the foundation for royal absolutism in France. He never once summoned the Estates General, and he implemented policies that helped to build the power of the monarch. Louis XIII, Option B, was a monarch who continued the process of consolidating absolute rule. Option C is incorrect because Louis XIV was known as the embodiment of an absolute monarch. He ruled longer than any other monarch in European history (1643–1715). During his rule, Louis consolidated political power in his hands by subordinating the nobility to his authority, building up a powerful army bent on expansion, revoking the rights of the Huguenots, exhibiting the glory and grandeur of his rule by constructing Versailles outside of Paris, and following mercantilist economic policies to finance his imperial ambitions.

157. (B) Philip V, the grandson of France's Louis XIV, was allowed to keep the throne in Spain as a result of the Peace of Utrecht, but he was forced to renounce his line of succession in the French line of succession. Option A is incorrect because, although the Hapsburgs gained the former Spanish possessions of Milan, Naples,

Sicily, and the Netherlands, they did not gain control over Spain proper, which went to Philip V. Option C is incorrect because what was eventually to become part of a unified Italy in 1861 was transferred to Austrian control. Option D is incorrect because close to the opposite occurred: the British added to their North American possessions largely at the expense of France.

158. (B) The United Provinces, also known as the Netherlands and Low Countries, were a personal union comprised of the kingdoms of the Netherlands, Belgium, the grand duchy of Luxemburg, a good portion of northern France, and a small part of western Germany. Option A is incorrect because it corresponds to largely eastern German lands. Option C is incorrect as it corresponds to the future United Kingdom, which is separated from mainland Europe by the English Channel. Option D is incorrect because these territories comprise Spain proper on the Iberian Peninsula.

159. (A) The three partitions of Poland at the end of the 18th century at the hands of Russia, Prussia, and Austria put an end to that state until 1918. Option B is incorrect because Poland was partitioned between Russia, Prussia, and Austria. Option C should have Prussia, not Hungary. Option D is incorrect as Lithuania was also partitioned away as a result of its union with Poland.

160. (A) The Pragmatic Sanction of 1713, issued by Austrian Hapsburg Emperor Charles VI, called on every diet in the empire and the various archdukes of the Hapsburg family to agree to the family's territory as indivisible and to recognize only one heir to the throne. The situation that prompted this edict was the absence of a male heir to succeed Charles VI.

161. (D) The Polish aristocracy, being the largest in Europe, was keen on preserving its substantial liberties from a strong absolute monarch. The aristocracy was able to control the power of the monarch by making that position an elected one. As a result, foreign influence became pervasive, and as Poland's absolutist neighbors Austria, Prussia, and especially Russia became more powerful, Poland's position weakened. This ultimately led to the three partitions of Poland that culminated with the elimination of the Polish state in 1796.

162. (C) Although the rise and expansion of Prussia in large measure was due to its powerful and disciplined military (Option D), this military power was based on land, not on sea. Options A, B, and D are factors in the rise and expansion of Prussia during the 17th and 18th centuries.

163. (B) Peter's construction of the city bearing his name (completed in 1703) was meant to be his "window on the West," symbolically reorienting his policies toward Western Europe, away from Moscow, which was located southeast of St. Petersburg. Option A is incorrect as Peter incorporated Baltic territories formerly belonging to Sweden as a result of the Treaty of Nystad, which ended the Great Northern War (1700–1721). Option C is incorrect. Although Peter's focus was to learn from the West to reform Russia, this did not stop Russian future expansion eastward. It was in the 19th century when the Russian Empire expanded farther southward into the Caucasus and eastward into the Central Asian Turkestan region, sparking an imperial competition with Great Britain. Option D is incorrect as Kiev had ceased to be Russia's capital since the 13th century.

164. **(C)** In the 18th century, although Russia made substantial territorial gains against both the Ottoman Empire (Option B) in southern Ukraine, the northern Caucasus, and the Crimean Peninsula, and Sweden (Option D) in the Baltic region as a result of the Treaty of Nystad, most of its gains were at the expense of Poland. During the three partitions of Poland between Russia, Prussia, and Austria, Russia regained control over Belarus, most of the Ukraine, and Lithuania.

165. **(C)** Poland's aristocracy, like in the Holy Roman Empire, was successful in preventing the centralization of political authority in the person of a strong monarch or in the institution of parliament. Monarchy in Poland was an elected position and although there was a central diet, it was too weak to make any decision affecting Poland as a whole, largely because of the infamous liberum veto, which allowed any member of the diet to stop an action if one person opposed that action. Instead, the aristocracy met in 50 to 60 regional diets, which prevented the unity of the country and allowed rising powers like Russia, Prussia, and Austria to gain substantial influence within the fractured Polish state.

166. **(A)** The Thirty Years' War (1618–1648) contributed to the rise of Sweden's power in Western Europe. The Swedish intervention in the Thirty Years' War is considered the turning point of the war. It helped the Protestant cause to win several major victories and established Sweden as an important Western European power. Option B is incorrect because it was as a result of its defeat in the Great Northern War (1700–1721) at the hands of Russia—and the subsequent Peace of Nystad that confirmed the loss of Estonia, Latvia, and southeast Finland—that Sweden lost its empire and its status as the dominant Baltic Sea power. Option C is incorrect as the Swedes did not take part in the War of the Spanish Succession (1700–1714). Option D is incorrect as the death of Charles XII while fighting in Denmark began a period of decline in Sweden's history.

167. **(A)** In return for aiding the Hapsburg Holy Roman Emperor in the War of the Spanish Succession, Frederick III of Prussia (Frederick I) became known as King Frederick I of Prussia. Option B is incorrect as the king of Prussia during the Seven Years' War (1756–1763) was Frederick II (Frederick the Great). Option C is incorrect as the French Revolution broke out in 1789. Option D is incorrect as the English Civil War preceded Frederick I's ascendancy to the Prussian throne by a half a century.

168. (A) Kiev, the capital of Ukraine, had been the capital and center of the first Russian state, known as Kievan Rus'. After the Mongol invasions, Kiev was destroyed in 1240. In the 14th century, Ukraine came under Lithuanian control. After the Treaty of Lublin in 1569, which officially unified Poland and Lithuania into a unified state, Ukraine came under Polish control. In 1648, Cossack leader Boghdan Khmelnitsky led an uprising of Orthodox Slavs against Polish rule that became successful after he asked for help from Russian Czar Alexei I. This resulted in parts of Ukraine becoming reintegrated into the Russian Empire. Finally, as a result of the three partitions of Poland in the late 18th century, most of Ukraine had been reincorporated into the Russian Empire.

169. (B) During Peter the Great's rule (1689–1725), Russia was at war for all but two years. The country's main foes were formidable: the Ottoman Turks to the south, who were blocking Russia's access to the Black Sea, and Sweden, which controlled the entire eastern shore of the Baltic Sea. To defeat the two militarily, Peter had to create a navy from scratch, invite foreign military experts to train his army, and reorganize his governing bureaucracy among other reforms he undertook.

170. (D) The Battle of Narva in 1700 was a great victory for Charles XII's Swedish forces over the Russians. However, Charles failed to deliver the final victory over Peter as he turned to secure his interests in Poland. Option A is incorrect because the Battle of Poltava of 1709 ended with the entire Swedish army under Charles XII destroyed. The Swedish king was able to escape to Ottoman Turkey, and Peter the Great's forces went on to conquer Livonia (Latvia) and eastern Finland. Option B is incorrect as the Battle of Kursk was fought in 1943 on the eastern front during World War II between the Soviet Red Army and the Nazi Wehrmacht and is known as the largest tank battle in history. Option C is incorrect as there was no Battle of Stockholm during the Great Northern War, although Russian troops did reach near the city.

171. (C) Liberty, equality, fraternity first appeared during the French Revolution. In December 1790 Robespierre advocated in a speech to the National Guards that the words "The French People and Liberty, Equality, Fraternity" be written on uniforms and flags, but his proposal was rejected. Nonetheless, the slogan was associated with the revolution until it was discarded during the empire.

172. (D) Lemaire is a French Canadian hockey player and former coach of the New Jersey Devils. All the other options refer to real French statesmen who proposed various reforms of the French financial system.

173. (B) When convened, the Estates General voted by estate. Usually, the First Estate, made up of clergy, and the Second Estate, comprised of the nobility, outvoted the Third Estate, which included the rest of the French population, by a two-to-one margin. Delegates from the Third Estate to the Estates General in 1789 proposed altering the system to a one person/one vote procedure, but the idea was rejected, prompting the delegates from the Third Estate to declare themselves in favor of a constitution.

174. (A) It is debatable whether the reformers who created the Declaration of the Rights of Man and Citizen had females in mind when producing this historic document. There is no explicit mention of women or women's rights anywhere in the document. Although progressive in its nature, it apparently didn't go far enough for Olympe de Gouges, who believed that the declaration was not being applied to women. This prompted her to write in 1791 her own manifesto for women's rights, the Declaration of the Rights of Woman and Citizen.

175. (D) Militant members of the Third Estate went to the Bastille to procure weapons to defend themselves from what they felt was an imminent attack from the royal forces. They were denied entry by the prison guards, who then fired at the demonstrators when they pushed forward into the prison yard. Almost 100 people were killed in the violence, the first of its magnitude in the French Revolution. This has been acknowledged as the beginning of the French Revolution.

176. (A) Louis and the National Assembly were brought to Paris by radical women and elements of the newly formed prorevolutionary National Guard. The move signified an increased distrust for the ruling family by the radicalized supporters of the revolution.

177. (D) In the context of the French Revolution, émigrés were nobles and aristocrats that opposed the revolution and fled France. Many organized opposition to the revolution from countries like Austria. Because this is a French word meaning "to migrate out," Options A, B, and C are incorrect.

178. (C) Russia did not join in the coalitions against France until 1798 after France had aroused the anger of the European powers by creating the Cisalpine Republic, the Roman Republic, and the Helvetic Republic. Option A is incorrect because Austria was one of the first countries that France declared war on during the French Revolution (April 20, 1792). Options B and D are also incorrect because both Great Britain and Holland joined Austria in forming the first coalition against France after the French Revolution's leaders executed Louis, opened the Scheldt estuary, and issued a decree offering assistance to all peoples wishing to be liberated.

179. (D) This answer is correct because it is the one exception to all of the other accurate options. There was no evidence of mass desertions that adversely affected the fighting ability of the anti-French coalition.

180. (C) In 1788 the French government devoted about 25 percent of its annual expenditures to maintain the armed forces. Military expenditures contributed most to the debt of all countries in Europe. Besides maintaining current armies and navies, another significant portion of the public debt came from the cost of past wars. Option A is incorrect because the upkeep of the royal court only accounted for 5 percent of public expenditures in France in 1788.

181. (D) At the dawn of the French Revolution, delegates of the Third Estate took it upon themselves to establish a legislative body that came to be called the National Assembly. These Third Estate delegates were soon joined by most delegates of the First Estate and some of the delegates for the Second Estate. With the support of the people, the National Assembly established a representative government with three separate and equal branches. Option A is incorrect. The Tennis Court Oath was an oath taken by deputies of the Third Estate when they met at a tennis court in defiance of King Louis XVI's order to disperse. The oath was an agreement not to disband until a new French constitution had been adopted. Option B is incorrect as the Réveillon riots grew from protests over rumors of lower wages for factory workers. These riots were one of the first instances of violence in the French Revolution. Option C is also incorrect. The guillotine became the main method of execution during the radical phase of the French Revolution. Among its most notable victims were Louis XVI; his wife, Marie Antoinette; and Maximilien Robespierre.

182. (B) Louis XVI was put on trial at that meeting of the National Convention, where ultimately the decision to execute him was made. Option A is incorrect. The formation of the French Constitution occurred in 1791. Option C is incorrect because the storming of the Tuileries by working-class Parisians happened spontaneously in August 1792. Option D is incorrect because it was on August 4, 1789, that a small group of liberal noblemen in the National Assembly surrendered their hunting rights, their rights in manorial courts, and feudal and seigneurial privileges in general. This paved the way for the Declaration of the Rights of Man and of the Citizen, issued less than three weeks later, which enshrined the principles of the rule of law, equal citizenship, and collective sovereignty of the people.

183. (A) The Civil Constitution of the Clergy of 1790 stipulated a number of points that brought the church under state authority. Among these points were: all clergy received salaries from the state; the church was prohibited from acknowledging any papal authority without government permission; and parish priests and bishops were to be elected by the voting-eligible citizenry, including non-Catholics.

184. (D) The Vatican condemned the Civil Constitution of the Clergy as an infringement on the rightful duties of the Catholic Church. As a result, relations between the French revolutionaries and the pro-Vatican and "refractory" elements of the French Catholic Church were hostile. All other options were measures taken by the revolutionary government against the Catholic Church.

185. (B) Under the Constitution of 1791, the king had to share power with a newly established Legislative Assembly whose members were to be indirectly elected. Option A did not happen until the execution of Louis XVI in January 1793.

Option C is incorrect because the franchise was increased, but not to all citizens. Option D was not part of the constitution.

186. (C) Robespierre presided over the period of the French Revolution known as the "Reign of Terror." During this radical phase of the revolution, Robespierre attempted to eliminate real and perceived enemies of the revolution. About 40,000 people were executed during this time. But by July 1794 Robespierre was executed by members of the Committee of Public Safety who felt Robespierre had lost the right to lead the revolution.

187. (A) Robespierre, arguably the leader of the Jacobins, had called for universal suffrage in 1789. The Jacobins were also strongly in favor of not only executing Louis XVI for treason but abolishing monarchy as a form of government in France. As radical as the Jacobins were, they generally did not seriously pursue policies that could be described as feminist or socialist as described in Options B and C. Although the Jacobins did believe that the revolution in France could only succeed if it was spread throughout Europe, they stopped with the continent. Finally, although the Jacobins did abolish slavery in Haiti in 1794, they stopped short of granting the colony independence.

188. (B) Marquis de Sade was a writer, nobleman, and revolutionary politician. He published erotic works that combined pornography with philosophical discourse. These tracts included blasphemy against Christianity. The words "sadist" and "sadism" are derived from his name. Options A, C, and D are incorrect. Napoleon Bonaparte was famous for his great love for his wife, Josephine; Maximilien Robespierre was the leader who advocated the use of terror to promote the virtuous goals of the revolution; and Jacques Necker was the finance minister for Louis XVI who tried unsuccessfully to curb the king's spending.

189. (C) European countries remembered the expansionist goals of the French king Louis XIV and welcomed the instability that detracted the country from pursuing an active foreign policy on the continent. On the other hand, with the radicalization of the revolution, the fear among the conservative monarchs was that the "contagion" of the revolution would spread to their countries and threaten the political order there.

190. (B) The sansculottes (so named because they did not wear upper-class breeches), the French working class in a preindustrial age, helped radicalize the revolution with their militancy and their demands for equality, direct democracy, a vigorous pursuit of revolutionary war against France's conservative enemies, and sworn opposition to the monarchy.

191. (C) The sans-culottes were arguably the "muscle" of the radical phase of the revolution. They were the common people of the lower class and made up the bulk of the Revolution's army during the early years of the revolution. Option A is incorrect as throughout the revolution the bourgeoisie provided not the muscle but the intellectual leadership. It was the bourgeois representatives to the National Assembly that drew up the Declaration of the Rights of Man and of the Citizen, the Civil Constitution of the Clergy, and the Constitution of 1791. Option B is incorrect because after the initial desire to convene the Estates General and a handful of nobles agreeing to "abolish feudalism," the nobility opposed the revolution. Option D is incorrect because the royal family opposed the revolution.

192. (A) The Haitian Revolution, inspired by the upheavals in France, led to the abolition of slavery on the island as well as independence. It was the second country in the Western Hemisphere to successfully establish its independence.

193. (D) All of the events listed contributed to the radicalization of the French Revolution. In Option A, the September Massacres of 1792 continued the chaotic violence unleashed by radicalized soldiers and workers in Paris a month earlier in the storming of the Tuileries royal palace, with more than 1,000 refractory priests and other counterrevolutionaries dragged from the prisons and massacred. In Option B, Louis XVI's execution for treason in 1793 brought an end to the Bourbon monarchy and resulted in the radical Committee of Public Safety coming to power with Maximilien Robespierre emerging as its leader. In Option C, the storming of the Tuileries resulted in the capture and arrest of King Louis XVI and his family. He was later convicted of treason and executed.

194. (D) About 70 percent of the 40,000 or so victims of the Reign of Terror were peasants and working people. Option A is incorrect as the nobles and clergy comprised about 8 percent and 6 percent of the total victims. Option B is incorrect as 14 percent of the victims were from the bourgeoisie. Option C is incorrect because the question implies the domestic victims of the political terror unleashed by the Committee of Public Safety, the government in control of France during the Reign of Terror.

195. (B) The Directory became increasingly unpopular from the political Left and Right in France from the time it came to power in 1795. Pro-Royalists who rallied around the dead king's brother, Louis XVIII, had supported his intentions to reinstate the Old Regime. On the Left, the Directory crushed an uprising known as the Conspiracy of Equals, a group that sympathized with the Jacobins and called for the abolition of private property. When the results of the elections in the spring of 1797 favored the pro-Royalist forces, the government annulled the election results. That September, the Directory called on Napoleon and his army to support the rule of the Directory. From this point until Napoleon's coup against the Directory in 1799, the army was the backbone of the Directory's ineffective rule.

196. (B) Although Napoleon Bonaparte was a strong supporter of the Jacobins who were the most vocal supporters of executing Louis XVI, he did not vote on whether to execute the king. Napoleon normalized relations with the Catholic

Church in Rome and French Catholics, Option A, and convinced many of the nobles who had fled France and actively opposed the revolution that they were needed in the country but that the clock would not be turned back to pre-1789 conditions, Option C. Napoleon's military prowess was undisputable from his early victories in France's revolutionary wars and this fact, coupled with his intelligence, his desire to preserve the gains of the revolution, and his goal to make France (and himself) bask in power and glory contributed to his extreme popularity during this period, Option D.

197. (D) Bonaparte crowned himself emperor of France on December 2, 1804. He had already proclaimed himself emperor in May of that year, but in December, at a coronation ceremony, he took the crown from the pope's hands and placed it on his own head. Option A is incorrect. The Tennis Court Oath was made on June 20, 1789, by delegates of the Third Estate concerning the establishment of a constitution. Bonaparte was not a part of this. Option B is also incorrect as Bonaparte was not involved in the early years of the Revolution, and Louis XVI was executed years before in 1793. Option C is incorrect because although Bonaparte was a key player in the coup that overthrew the Directory, that event occurred in 1799.

198. (D) Napoleon had favored quick, decisive battles as well as living off the occupied country's own supplies. Given the vast expanses of Russia, Czar Alexander I could afford to retreat deep into the Russian heartland, overexposing Napoleon's supply lines. Napoleon reached Moscow in September 1812, but the city was desolate and soon to be in flames. Shortly afterward, Napoleon began his disastrous retreat, which eventually cost him more than 500,000 men.

199. (C) Napoleon Bonaparte was born in Corsica in 1769 into a family of minor nobles.

200. (C) The code did not grant privileges to any groups, especially the aristocracy, as this would have run counter to the ideals of the French Revolution. Napoleon was a strong supporter of the French Revolution because without the revolution, he, as a Corsican from minor nobility, would have never risen to ranks as high as he did in the French Army and, later, in French politics. The Napoleonic Code reflects the revolutionary ideals that he supported.

201. (C) The Continental System was an economic embargo of British trade devised by Napoleon and imposed on his satellites and allies with the intention of weakening Great Britain economically. The Continental System was ultimately a failure for a number of reasons. First, the British carried on substantial commerce with its overseas colonies, so the loss of continental European trade did not significantly impact the health of the British economy. Second, the Continental System caused wide-scale resentment toward Napoleon and his regime among the occupied countries as well as allies such as Russia. Third, the Continental System financially wrecked some of the European commercial bourgeoisie who were heavily dependent on overseas trade.

202. (B) The Battle of Trafalgar was a naval engagement fought between the British Royal Navy and the French and Spanish navies. In approximately five hours, the British devastated Napoleon's forces. Option A is incorrect, although Napoleon's campaign against the Russians was his costliest in terms of manpower and materials. Napoleon's forces lost more than 500,000 men in their retreat from Moscow, as bitterly cold winter conditions and determined Russian forces pursued the Grand Armée westward out of Russia and into Europe. However, the Russian campaign did not affect France's naval dominance. Options C and D are also incorrect. Waterloo was Napoleon's final defeat, but not of naval significance, and the Battle of Austerlitz was a great victory for Napoleon.

203. (B) Russia formally withdrew from the Continental System in 1810 and resumed commercial relations with Great Britain. This angered Napoleon and convinced him that an invasion of his former ally was necessary to teach Alexander I a lesson.

204. (C) Ever since the Third Partition of Poland in 1795, Poles pinned their hopes on revolutionary France to gain their state back. Napoleon created the Duchy of Warsaw in 1807, and many Poles fought in the Grand Armée. More than 90,000 fought in Napoleon's Russian campaign.

205. (C) The major powers at the Congress of Vienna wanted to prevent any attempts by France to spread its influence beyond its borders. To that end, the Congress implemented a series of measures to contain France. Among those measures were to revive the Dutch Republic and transform it into the kingdom of Holland, adding to that country Belgium. The Italian kingdom of Piedmont was restored and strengthened by adding the defunct Republic of Genoa to it. All Bonapartes that were put in power by Napoleon, including Napoleon himself, were forced to leave, replaced by the former monarchs or their offspring.

206. (A) The Dutch Republic was a leading banking center in Europe until the French Revolution. The Bank of Amsterdam, founded in 1609, accepted deposits from all over the world. The Dutch government guaranteed the safety of these deposits, which contributed to the popularity of the bank. During the 17th century, the Dutch dominated commercial shipping in Europe. They also expanded their trade beyond Europe. In 1619 they established the city of Batavia in Java; they were the only Europeans allowed by the Japanese to establish a presence in Japan for two centuries; and they established settlements in both North (Manhattan Island) and south (Brazil, Caracas, Curacao, Guiana) America. Options B and C are incorrect because these industries didn't exist in Holland during this time, while Option D is incorrect because, although the Dutch were innovators in agricultural production, the economy rested on maritime trade, banking, and finance.

207. (A) Mercantilism was characterized by state regulation of trade in order to increase the state's power against its neighbors and rivals. Option B is incorrect because the merchants had little independence to initiate economic policy. Economic policy was usually determined by a finance minister intent on strengthening the state. Option C is incorrect because free trade was antithetical to the principles of mercantilism. Option D is incorrect as labor was very immobile at the time.

208. (C) Dutch banks did charge interest on loans but much lower than French or English banks. All of the other options are true and are all factors that contributed to the Dutch Republic's prosperity during the 17th century.

209. (D) Holland, which was one of the provinces that eventually comprised the Dutch Republic, gained its independence from Spain in 1648 as a result of the Thirty Years' War and the Peace of Westphalia. This was the culmination of 80 years of rebellion by the Dutch against Spanish rule. The other options were contributing factors to the success of the Dutch Republic during the 17th century.

210. (A) The Navigation Acts were a series of laws the English Parliament passed that prohibited foreign trade with its colonial possessions. These acts primarily targeted the supremacy of Dutch commercial shipping, which had dominated trade on the Iberian Peninsula in 1647, the Mediterranean, the Baltic, and even with English colonies. The result was three wars between the English and the Dutch from 1652 to 1674 during which the English annexed New Amsterdam and renamed it New York.

211. (B) Colbert actually lowered internal tariffs in a large portion of the country by creating an internal free-trade zone the size of England called the Five Great Farms. The remaining options are all measures Colbert undertook to strengthen the French economy so that Louis XIV could reorganize and enlarge his army, construct Versailles, and accommodate the growing bureaucracy necessary to help administer the growing state.

212. (B) Finance Minister Colbert did not establish a central bank in France. He did encourage the manufacture of silks, tapestries, glasswares, woolens, uniforms, and weapons for Louis XIV's army. He built roads and canals, created the French East India Company, and built up the navy to encourage overseas commerce and colonization.

213. (B) In 1609 the Dutch established the Bank of Amsterdam, which became the most important and most reliable financial institution in all of Europe. Deposits were guaranteed by the Dutch government, and the bank attracted capital from all parts of Europe, making it possible to make loans for various purposes. Ultimately, in the 18th and 19th centuries, London becomes the financial center of Europe by virtue of Great Britain's leading role in the Industrial Revolution.

214. (A) Jamaica became a British colony in 1655 when the British captured it from Spain. The conflict between Britain and Spain was finally resolved in 1670 with the signing of the Treaty of Madrid. As part of the terms of that treaty, Spain relinquished its claim on Jamaica. Option B is incorrect as Anglo-Dutch forces seized Gibraltar in 1704, and the British retained possession of it as a result of the Treaty of Utrecht in 1713. Option C is incorrect as the French forfeited their claims to Canada to the British in 1763 as a result of the Treaty of Paris that ended the Seven Years' War. Option D is incorrect as India became a direct possession of the British crown in 1858 in response to the failed Sepoy uprising against the rule of the British East India Company.

215. (D) Aristocratic men with an interest in science received subsidies from the English government to pursue their scientific interests. Option A is incorrect because the Royal Society of London had nothing to do with arts and culture. It was strictly limited to the pursuit of science. Option B is incorrect because although most people who received a government charter to pursue scientific study were nobles, the Royal Society did not ennoble men. Option C is incorrect because the organization had nothing to do with military affairs.

216. (A) A flu vaccine was not developed until the 20th century. Option B is at the core of the Scientific Revolution. Option C may have been invented in the 16th century, but its first practical application was in the 17th century. In Option D, Edward Jenner developed the vaccine for smallpox in 1795.

217. (C) Dimitry Mendeleyev was a Russian scientist who was passionate about chemistry. His biggest scientific contribution was the periodic table of elements, which he developed in 1869. Option A is incorrect because Kepler's contributions were in astronomy and mathematics. Option B is incorrect, although Leibniz did contribute to the world some original understandings of calculus. Option D is incorrect, although Newton is recognized as one of the most influential scientists of all time.

218. (A) The use of reason, logic, and scientific inquiry were at the heart of the revolution in science. Philosophes of the Enlightenment believed these methods of thinking and inquiry could also be applied to government to improve how people are governed. Option B is incorrect because there was no confirmation of a supreme being during this time. Option C is incorrect because there was no correlation between separation of political power and the laws of nature. Option D is incorrect because the Scientific Revolution did have a major influence on the Enlightenment because the two movements shared the same emphasis on reason and logic.

219. (A) The center of the Enlightenment was Paris, France, where philosophers and educated elites from France and other European countries gathered in salons to exchange ideas. France was also the home of the most influential Enlightenment thinkers: Voltaire, Rousseau, Montesquieu, and Diderot. Option B is incorrect. Although England could boast of John Locke, Adam Smith, David Ricardo, and others, England was not a gathering place of Enlightenment thinkers. Option C is incorrect. Although Voltaire for a time lived in Potsdam at the invitation of Fredrick the Great, not many other thinkers were attracted to Prussia like Paris. Option D is incorrect. Enlightenment ideas reached Russia in the late 18th century under Catherine the Great, who corresponded with Diderot and Voltaire. But Russia did not attract the Enlightenment thinkers from the West.

220. (A) Hobbes, an Englishman, had limited appeal in his own country. His views were well received in absolutist countries in Europe, albeit not well publicized, since the Bible and religion had little influence on his work. Option B is incorrect because Locke was a much bigger influence on the philosophy behind the American Revolution than Hobbes's support for absolutism. Option C is incorrect because he didn't have much faith in people to participate in a democratic government. Option D is incorrect because his work had nothing in common with the works of Karl Marx, the originator of the concept of "scientific Socialism."

221. (D) All of the options are factors that contributed to the consolidation of absolutist rule in Russia by Peter the Great. In Option A, Peter's creation of the Table of Ranks gave him control over the status of individuals in Russia, control that he didn't have when rank and status were based on heredity. In Option B, the construction of St. Petersburg, similar to the construction of Versailles by French king Louis XIV, was done to gather important nobles to live in one place under the watchful eye of the monarch. Both Peter and Louis also had bad childhood experiences with political intrigues in their respective capital cities, which had an impact on their decisions to construct new glorious cities. In Option C, the abolition of the position of patriarch by Peter and its replacement with a committee of bishops known as the Holy Synod, chaired by a civilian official known as the Procurator, was Peter's way of gaining administrative control of the powerful Russian Orthodox Church.

222. (B) The Time of Troubles (1598–1613) saw the Russian state threatened with disintegration as a succession crisis triggered the biggest crisis in Russian history since the Mongol conquest and occupation. During the Time of Troubles, boyars fought amongst themselves, the lower classes revolted against their growing bondage, and foreign armies occupied Moscow. It was this situation that led many to conclude that czarist absolutism was necessary to restore order and unity to the Russian state. Hobbes's writings gave structure and theory to those who supported absolutism as a force for order.

223. (C) Written constitutions became a central demand of Enlightenment thinkers of the 18th and 19th centuries to limit the power of monarchs and to define the rights of citizens; therefore, constitutions were antithetical to absolute rule. The other options were necessary characteristics of absolute rule.

224. (B) Delegates to the Estates General from the Third Estate formed the National Assembly in June 1789 with the intent to create a constitution for France. When they were locked out of the meeting place of the Estates General, the delegates moved to a tennis court nearby and pledged to not disband until a constitution was established. This oath was a rejection of the absolutist nature of the French state (Option A). Option C is incorrect because the overwhelming majority of those pledging the oath were members of the Third Estate, while the clergy comprised the First Estate. Option D is incorrect because, although the French Revolution will enter a more radical phase characterized by the period known as the "Reign of Terror," this was not the original intention of those delegates pledging allegiance to the Tennis Court Oath.

225. (C) Montesquieu is known for his emphasis on the separation of power in government. In his publication *Spirit of the Laws*, he argued that the best way to prevent despotism, the primary threat in any government, was to create a separation of power. Option A is incorrect because Hobbes rejected the idea of separation of powers. Option B is incorrect as Rousseau was known for his philosophy of a "general will." In *The Social Contract* (1762), Rousseau wrote that the general will, or a set of common interests that citizens possess or should possess, serves as the foundation for a government's legitimacy. Option D is incorrect because Kant was a German philosopher whose works focused primarily on the human intellect and the place of reason in human thought.

226. (C) Voltaire admired absolutist monarchs such as Louis XIV of France and Frederick the Great of Prussia for their promotion of art, literature, and science. Voltaire cared less about political liberty and more about a leader who was an "enlightened despot," who promoted progress while reigning in the power of official churches. Option A is incorrect for a number of reasons but primarily because a representative government, elected by men and women, was a progressive idea even beyond Voltaire's imagination. Option B is incorrect because Voltaire rejected any political power that rested on divine explanations as superstitious and regressive. Option D is incorrect because neither Voltaire nor any of the major Enlightenment philosophers called for a direct form of democracy.

227. (C) Rousseau believed that people could attain the "general will" by creating laws that they would live by together. Therefore, the social contract was between the people themselves. Rousseau advocated popular sovereignty over monarchy and religious toleration instead of an official church. This is why Option A is incorrect. Option B is incorrect because he saw the "government"—magistrates and governing officials—as carrying out the policies developed by the people. Option D is incorrect because Rousseau's main concept in *The Social Contract* is the general will, and the general will is meant to include all people, regardless of class background.

228. (C) Locke believed that people were born with certain "natural rights." These rights were life, liberty, and property. Locke believed in a "social contract" between governed and government. The people would give up their "state of nature" to a government that they have chosen in order for that government to protect the rights of all. Government's biggest responsibility is to ensure the natural rights of its citizens. Option A is incorrect because this is Copernicus's theory. Option B is incorrect because, although the concept of universal suffrage and the welfare state are outgrowths of Enlightenment thinking, these were late 19th- and early 20th-century concepts, still premature for Locke's time. Option D is incorrect because this concept is closely related to Socialism or Communism.

229. (A) Rene Descartes is alternately known as the "father of rationalism" and the "father of modern philosophy."

230. (B) Mary Wollstonecraft's most influential work was *Vindication of the Rights of Woman*, published in 1792.

231. (B) Voltaire denounced the Catholic Church primarily because he felt that it was a bulwark against progress and "enlightenment." Voltaire was a harsh critic of censorship, and the Catholic Church's Index of Forbidden Books banned many of the great works of western art, science, philosophy, and literature. Voltaire was a major supporter of science and scientific inquiry. Option A is incorrect because Voltaire admired Great Britain as among the freest countries in the world. Option C is incorrect because Voltaire carried on correspondence with Catherine, referring to her as "the star of the North." Option D is incorrect because at the invitation of Fredrick (the Great), Voltaire moved to Potsdam. There was a strong mutual admiration between the two.

232. (A) Although being reform minded, enlightened despots did not surrender to limits on their political powers as absolute monarchs. Options B through D are incorrect as all are characteristic reforms of enlightened despots.

233. (A) Since the home of the Enlightenment was France and most aristocrats in Europe preferred speaking French, French was the "lingua franca" of Europe during the 18th century. Option B is incorrect because German was largely confined to the German-speaking territories of the Holy Roman Empire and Prussia. Option C is incorrect because English would become the dominant international language thanks to the extent of British imperialism, but not as yet during the Enlightenment. Option D is incorrect because French superseded Spanish in Europe.

234. (C) This answer is best illustrated in Maximilien Robespierre's February 1794 speech, *On Virtue and Terror*. In the speech, virtue, which is defined as love of country, its laws, and equality, is the "fundamental principle of democratic or popular government," i.e., virtue is the "general will."

235. (C) Liberals generally favored constitutional monarchy and the more moderate phase of the revolution. Conservatives opposed the revolution from the outset and favored the old order prior to 1789. Republicans favored the radical Jacobin phase of the French Revolution. They favored the abolition of monarchy.

236. (C) Louis XIV required the nobles to live at Versailles to keep them away from politics and to keep watch over them. Option A is incorrect since the middle class, which was quite small at that time, showed no tendencies to rebel against the monarch. Option B is incorrect because the peasants were denied a voice in politics and were generally not considered worthy of enjoying the life at Versailles. Option D is incorrect because the clergy was also a trusted estate by Louis.

237. (D) Russia. Rather than a distinct social group, Russian nobility felt they were the servants of the czar.

238. (C) The peasantry, the largest segment of the Third Estate, bore the majority of the tax burden in France prior to the outbreak of the revolution in 1789. This was one of the causes of the French Revolution. The landed nobility of the Second Estate, the clergy of the First Estate, and the monarchy were all exempt from paying taxes.

239. (A) The officer corps in European armies in the 18th century came largely from the landed aristocracy. Option B is incorrect because middle-class males rarely attained positions of leadership in militaries. Option C is incorrect because, unlike in the 15th and 16th centuries, mercenaries were no longer used because of their questionable reliability. Option D is incorrect because the peasants almost always comprised the rank-and-file soldiers

240. (C) Until the Industrial Revolution in Europe, which began in Great Britain in the mid-18th century and in the 19th century in most other Western European states, the peasants made up the overwhelming majority of the population. For example, on the eve of the French Revolution, peasants constituted about 76 percent of the population. But the farther east one went in Europe (Poland, Russia), the peasant population approached 90 percent.

241. (A) The nobility in all European countries except Poland rarely exceeded 5 percent of the population. Poland had the largest percentage of nobles with 8 percent.

242. (D) The Polish aristocracy in the 17th century comprised about 8 percent of the country's population, the highest proportion in Europe.

243. (A) Spending on the military was typically the largest expenditure (excluding payment of debt) that the 18th-century state incurred. Option B, spending on royal palaces, although costly, did not match expenditures on the military. The remaining options are not correct because 18th-century governments typically spent very little on education, anything that could be identified with welfare programs, or even infrastructure projects. Such government programs were not a mainstay feature of European nations until the 20th century.

244. (B) In the 17th century, the measure of wealth was in land ownership (Option C), not one's possession of cash or capital, which was becoming more commonplace but not yet a dominating factor as it would be in industrial Europe after the 19th century. Options A and D were signs of high social status in Europe during the 17th century.

245. (A) The ethnic majority of the Austrian Hapsburg Empire was the Slavic people. They were comprised of Poles, Serbs, Czechs, Slovaks, Slovenes, and Croats. Option B, although seemingly the obvious choice, is incorrect as the Austrian and other ethnically Germanic people were outnumbered by the more numerous Slavs. Option C is incorrect as while there were Italians in the emerging Austrian Empire, they were not very numerous. Option D is incorrect as the Magyars (Hungarians) grew in number and ultimately co-ruled the empire after 1867 but did not comprise the mathematical majority in the Austrian and Austro-Hungarian Empire.

246. (B) Under Peter the Great, the nobility was forced to serve the state: virtually all landowning and serf-owning aristocrats were required to serve in the army or civil administration. The bureaucracy was increased to accommodate the growth in service requirements. Options A, C, and D reflect the condition of the Russian nobility under Peter the Great.

247. (A) Urban workers suffered the most from the rise in food prices because they relied on the peasants in the countryside to provide food to the cities. Peasants horded food rather than sell it for depreciating prices.

248. (B) The Second Estate was made up of the French aristocracy. These were nobles with titles such as Duc, Comte, and Viscomte. Options A and C are incorrect because the First Estate was made up exclusively of the clergy, while the Third Estate consisted of the bourgeoisie, or middle class, as well as urban workers and peasants. Option D is incorrect because émigrés were people who had come from other countries to live in France.

249. (C) The bourgeoisie were the wealthiest, best-educated, and most active force behind the French Revolution. Option A is incorrect as the sans-culottes—who were largely the poor working class such as shopkeepers, tradespeople, artisans, and factory workers primarily in Paris—were politically significant but not the driving force of the Revolution. They were, however, considered the backbone of the Revolution and at one time made up a large portion of the army. Option B is incorrect because, although the peasants comprised about 90 percent of France's population in 1789, they were not as instrumental in causing the uprising.

Period 3

250. (C) In 1815, Parliament, dominated by the gentry, passed the Corn Laws, which raised the protective tariff to the benefit of landlords and their farmers.

251. (C) The repeal of the Corn Laws of 1846 symbolized the ascendancy of industrial interests over agricultural. The Corn Laws placed high protective tariffs on grain imports, hurting the British working class. To prevent uprisings of the workers, industrialists were forced to raise wages, keeping the cost of production up, resulting in more expensive products that hurt their exports. By repealing the Corn Laws, Britain became dependent on its industries for its economic power and imports of agricultural supplies.

252. (C) The Corn Laws were passed for the benefit of the nobility and other large landowners. These laws were a group of tariffs imposed on grain grown in England. These tariffs protected the grain prices from foreign competition and forced people to pay higher prices. Option A is incorrect as the Corn Laws hampered manufacturers' expansion. Options B and D are also incorrect as the Corn Laws did not benefit and were actually detrimental to the working class because it caused the price of their food to increase.

253. (B) A series of successful inventions in the textile industry such as John Kay's flying shuttle, the spinning jenny, and Richard Arkwright's water frame required many workers to operate them and large buildings where these large machines could be gathered. This led to the establishment of the first factories.

254. (C) The colonial empire that Britain built in Latin America and India, and later in Africa, along with its dominant position in the slave trade, provided an important market for British goods. Option A is incorrect because the British guarded their industrial production from outsiders as long as they could. Options B and D are incorrect because at the outset of the Industrial Revolution, British factory owners were setting up factories exclusively in Britain. Wages were low enough in Britain so that there wasn't a need to establish factories and export jobs to the colonies.

255. (C) Although Britain's supply of key natural resources like iron and coal were abundant, the country was not diverse in the resources that it possessed. All of the other options are factors that contributed to the Industrial Revolution in Britain, plus the fact that there were no internal tariffs

256. (A) The first large factories in the British Industrial Revolution were in the cotton textile industry. A series of successful inventions in the textile industry, such as John Kay's flying shuttle, the spinning jenny, and Richard Arkwright's water frame, required many workers to operate them and large buildings to accommodate these large machines. This led to the establishment of the first factories.

257. (A) As a result of these inventions, cotton production was 10 times higher in 1790 than it was in 1770. Option B is incorrect because the opposite occurred. With the invention of new technology that sped up the production of textile-based products, factories were established to accommodate the new production reality. In Option C, the new inventions did give rise to a new type of energy source, but the solution was not yet oil, it was steam. In Option D, the inventions that led to increased production in textile-based products may have had some distant effect on the production of faster ships, but the link is not as strong as in Option A.

258. (C) The goal of the enclosure movement was not to collectivize land. Collectivization of agricultural land was an important policy of Joseph Stalin and the Soviet Communist Party of the late 1920s to 1930s. If anything, the enclosure movement was the complete opposite of collectivization. The hundreds of enclosure acts passed by a British Parliament dominated by large landowners in the 17th and 18th centuries fenced in open fields in villages and divided the common land in proportion to one's property in the open fields.

259. (A) Charles Townshend introduced to England the four-crop rotation that he learned from Dutch farmers when he was Britain's ambassador to that country. The four-crop rotation (wheat, barley, a root crop, and clover) replaced the three-field system in which two fields were used to grow and one would remain fallow so as to not drain the soil of all of its nutrients. Option B is incorrect. Although he also was known to use abundant manure in fertilizing his own fields upon return to England, he is not known as the pioneer of this agricultural practice. Neither is he associated with the agricultural innovations mentioned in Options C and D.

260. (D) The putting-out system is where the merchant provided (put out) raw materials to several cottage workers, who processed the raw materials in their homes and returned the finished products to the merchant. Although the putting-out system, like the factory system that eventually replaced it, ended up producing a variety of goods, both types of production began largely with textile-based finished goods.

261. (A) The Crystal Palace Exhibition, also known as the Great Exhibition, was organized by members of the Royal Society of the Arts. The purpose of this exhibition was for Great Britain to demonstrate its industrial leadership, not for skilled artisans to stave off industrialization of their craft, as Option D states. Option B is incorrect because crystal was not the focus of this exhibition. Option C is incorrect because although the bourgeoisie may have used the exhibition as an opportunity to "show off" their wealth, that was not the main idea behind the exhibition.

262. (B) The Crystal Palace is considered the first prefabricated building. Paxton divided the design into modules that could be fully supported by themselves so that the building could be put together rapidly. Option A is incorrect as after the Great Exhibition, the palace was moved to another site where it was used for shows and other events. Option C is also incorrect as the palace took less than nine months to build. Option D is incorrect as the Crystal Palace became the standard, and other exhibitions and fairs were held in similar buildings.

263. (A) Prince Albert envisioned the exhibition as a way for the wonders of industry from all over the world to be displayed, although it was also a chance for Britain to show off its industrial advances. Many other countries had exhibitions there. This, of course, means Option D is inaccurate. Options B and C are also incorrect. More than six million people attended the exhibition, and it was a rousing financial success, with a profit of more than GBP 186,000.

264. (D) The Zollverein was a tariff union between the various German states first implemented in 1834. The Zollverein facilitated trade among member German states by allowing goods to move tariff-free while erecting a single tariff against other nations. Besides helping develop the economies of the German Zollverein members, this economic union was seen as a significant step toward the creation of a unified German state in 1871.

265. (B) Louis Napoleon was known for his domestic policy, which promoted public works and established social welfare programs. Unfortunately for him, his domestic policies did not prevent his defeat in the Franco-German War and the subsequent uprising in France, during which he was deposed. Option A is incorrect as Charles X was known as an ultraroyalist and defender of the royal prerogative. He was not known for his support of public works and social welfare. Option C is incorrect also, as Louis-Eugene Cavaignac is actually known for his harsh acts against Parisian workers. Option D is also incorrect as Louis Philippe was known for his unwillingness to address the political and social problems in the country.

266. (A) Cotton-based clothing became much cheaper and more affordable for the masses. Prior to the Industrial Revolution, only the wealthy could afford the comfort and cleanliness of underwear because it was made from expensive linen cloth. Option B is incorrect because, with few exceptions, Great Britain had a steady supply of cotton from its North American colonies or India. Option C is incorrect because the opposite took place: India's textile industry (not industry in the modern sense) was destroyed by the innovations in textile production developed in Great Britain. Option D is incorrect because the opposite was true: working conditions in the textile factories were terrible, with the exploitation of child labor a common occurrence.

267. (C) As a result of Watt's steam engine, inventors and engineers could devise and implement all kinds of power equipment to aid people in their work.

268. (D) The development of the railroad and railroad transportation in Britain in the 19th century was revolutionary for the factors listed in Options A through C. The opposite of Option D actually occurred. Because coal replaced wood as the main energy source for steam engines, the expansion of the network of railroads in Britain and other industrializing nations led to the growth of coal production.

269. (C) The effect of the rapid increase in population in Britain from 1780 to 1851 is a controversial topic among historians, and no consensus has been found among them. On the one hand, while the British economy rose fourfold, the world population more than doubled and the average per person consumption rose only by 75 percent. On the other hand, historians argue that the rapid population growth was actually helpful because it facilitated industrial expansion because of a larger industrial workforce.

270. (B) The standard of living of British workers did not rise from 1792 to 1820. The Napoleonic Wars took a toll on the economies of the continental countries, and the British working class was not immune. Only after 1820, and especially after 1840, did real wages rise significantly, but so did the hours in the average worker's week. Option A is incorrect because although the Industrial Revolution had begun, it had not resulted in more leisure time for the working class. Options C and D are not true because workers did not begin working longer hours and earning more until after 1840.

271. (B) The Factory Act of 1833 limited the factory workday for children ages 9–13 to 8 hours and that of adolescents ages 14–18 to 12 hours. The act did not specify domestic labor or work in small businesses. Concerns for the environment, equal wages for women, and workman's compensation were not addressed by the act.

272. (A) The Mines Act, passed by the British Parliament in 1842, prohibited underground work for all women as well as for boys under the age of 10. Option B is incorrect because women had been working in coal mines long before the Mines Act. Options C and D are incorrect as there were no provisions made for work in mines during summer break or after school nor was there any mention of quotas.

273. (B) There was a drop in the number of deaths from famines, epidemics, and war. Major diseases such as plague and smallpox declined noticeably. Option A is incorrect as that time period witnessed conflicts on an international scale such as the Seven Years' War (1756–1763), the French Revolution and the Napoleonic Wars that followed (1789–1815), and several smaller conflicts. Option C is incorrect as immigration from Latin America and Africa to Europe was negligible. Option D is incorrect as the use of contraceptives was not widespread until the 20th century.

274. (C) Ireland's population doubled between 1781 and 1845. But as a result of the devastating potato famine that struck Ireland between 1845 and 1851, more than one million died of starvation and disease while almost two million migrated to the United States. All of the other countries listed experienced population growth.

275. (C) In 1800 Great Britain had one major city, London, with a population of one million, and six cities with a population of between 50,000 and 100,000. Fifty years later, London's population had soared to 2.3 million, while nine other cities had populations of more than 100,000.

276. (B) Most schools of the time did not offer religious instruction but left it to whatever church the family belonged. Option A is incorrect because often military training was included in schools, particularly for boys. Options C and D are incorrect because there was a belief that an educated citizenry would be both productive and less likely to succumb to poverty and being tyrannized by a despot.

277. (C) This is a quote from the Emancipation Reform of 1861 in Russia, the last country to free its serfs. Option A is incorrect as the pope did not make laws for serfs or anyone else. Options B and D are incorrect as they were in power after the serfs had been freed in their countries.

278. (C) No feminists of the 19th century would have dreamed about military service for women. Indeed, conscription for men was just becoming more common. Option A is incorrect because women could not own property before the women's rights movement. Options B and D are incorrect because there were unequal qualifications and standards regarding divorce and adultery for men and women.

279. (C) Oil will not be discovered in the Arabian Peninsula until the 1920s. All other options represent importing of goods that had been going on since at least the early 1800s, if not before.

280. (B) The Reform Act, passed by Parliament in 1832, introduced significant changes to the British electoral system to reflect the transformations brought on by the Industrial Revolution. For example, in addition to increasing the number of males who could vote from 500,000 to more than 800,000, the Reform Act redistributed suffrage rights by region and class. As a result, more seats in Parliament were made for industrial towns where middle-class factory owners, businessmen, doctors, lawyers, and bankers lived at the expense of seats for smaller older towns.

281. (D) Liberals were generally middle-class businessmen and professionals: lawyers, doctors, and bankers. They supported representative government, freedom of speech and the press, and religious tolerance, but they opposed extending democratic rights to all, fearing the possibility of mob rule. They supported laissez-faire economics and opposed the formation of labor unions.

282. (C) Robert Owen was a proponent of utopian socialism. He was also an advocate for factory workers, implementing many reforms, including the creation of communities for workers. He was regarded as the leader of labor unionism and in 1834 formed the Grand National Consolidated Trades Union, an organization established to represent all labor. This organization did not last long but created an enduring legacy for the union movement. Options A and B are incorrect. Karl Marx and Friedrich Engels are best known for their writing and publishing the Communist Manifesto. This work predicted an uprising of the proletarian class that would replace capitalism with socialism; it became the foundation of the modern communist movement. Option D is also incorrect. Charles Fourier was a utopian socialist best known for his book *The Social Destiny of Man*. In it, he lays forth a plan to create a socialist society.

283. (A) Edwin Chadwick, an urban reformer, published the Report in 1842. In it, he concluded that serious diseases and illnesses were caused by pollution, poor sanitary conditions, and overcrowded living conditions. He called for sanitary reforms including efficient sewers and improvements in the supply of clean water. Six years later the National Board of Health was created.

284. (D) Count Saint Simon is considered the original social reformer. He published many works on social reform and envisioned a future where "industrialization" (a term he coined) eliminated war and poverty. Option A is incorrect. Karl Marx is the founder of "scientific Socialism," which argues Socialism is the eventual result of proletarian revolution. Options B and C are also incorrect, although like Count Saint Simon, Robert Owen and Charles Fourier both tried to create small communes and other model communities.

285. (B) According to Engels's *Socialism: Utopian and Scientific*, published in 1880, his explanation for why his and Marx's version of Socialism is scientific can be summarized in the following passage: "The materialist conception of history starts from the proposition that the production of the means to support human life and, next to production, the exchange of things produced, is the basis of all social structure; that in every society that has appeared in history, the manner in which wealth is distributed and society divided into classes or orders is dependent upon what is produced, how it is produced, and how the products are exchanged. From this point of view, the final causes of all social changes and political revolutions are to be sought, not in men's brains, not in men's better insights into eternal truth and justice, but in changes in the modes of production and exchange. They are to be sought, not in the philosophy, but in the economics of each particular epoch."

286. (A) In *The Conditions of the Working Class in England in 1844*, Friedrich Engels blamed industrial capitalism for the extreme misery of the English proletariat's miserable living and working conditions. Engels, Karl Marx's longtime friend and ally, had managed to see firsthand the plight of the working class in Manchester. Marx and Engels recognized the productive capacity of capitalism and the progressive nature of it compared to feudalism, but neither lauded the system nor defended its exploitative nature, as Options B and C state. Option D is incorrect because both Marx and Engels believed capitalism was a higher stage of development than the agriculturally dominated economy of feudalism.

287. (A) In 1848, following the June Days in France, the Constituent Assembly decided to create a strong executive to be elected by universal male suffrage. The elections were held in December of that year, and Louis Napoleon Bonaparte, the nephew of the great Napoleon, won the election in a landslide.

288. (C) In the tumultuous 19th century, the British populace largely avoided revolution because of the factors mentioned in Options A, B, and D, plus the longstanding tradition of parliamentary representation. Universal suffrage and extensive social welfare programs would not be a reality in Great Britain until the 20th century.

289. (B) List believed that, in the case of the German states and other industrializing nations, protective tariffs were essential to support the development of domestic industries against more developed economies. He was critical of Britain's free-trade policies because he felt that this was Britain's way to reduce everyone else to dependency on it.

290. (D) The Luddites, active in England between 1811 and 1816, were named after Ned Ludd, a mythical figure who supposedly led the movement. The Luddites, who blamed unemployment on the mechanization of the textile industry, broke into factories and smashed power looms and wide weaving frames. Ultimately, the "movement" fizzled out on its own.

291. (D) The Combination Acts, first passed by the British Parliament in 1799, outlawed labor unions and strikes. Parliament repealed the acts in 1824 in the face of widespread working-class opposition to them.

292. (D) The Chartist movement was a working-class movement that got its name from the "People's Charter," which was an 1838 campaign for parliamentary reform of the political inequities arising from the Reform Act of 1832. The most important demand of the Chartists was universal male suffrage. The Chartists presented Parliament with three signed petitions with their demands between 1839 and 1848; one of them had more than three million signatures in 1842. All of them were rejected. After the final rejection in 1848, the movement ended.

293. (C) Kaiser Wilhelm II had an abiding love for ships, and he hoped a stronger navy would give Germany a better vantage from which to deal with Great Britain, the preeminent naval force of the time.

294. (C) Liberalism was a belief in individualism, free trade and commercial development, and constitutionalism. This would benefit the bourgeoisie most, as it would protect and develop business under a strong legal footing. Option A is incorrect as peasant and worker representation were not usually included among liberal demands. Options B and D are incorrect because these classes were already represented in the old order.

295. (B) In *The Eighteenth Brumaire of Louis Bonaparte*, published four years after *The Communist Manifesto*, Karl Marx referred to the June Days, also known as the June Insurrection of 1848, as "the most colossal event in the history of European civil wars." In his analysis, the crushing of the proletarian insurrection was an example of the ruthless struggle of the bourgeoisie against the assertion of the interests of the proletariat class.

296. (C) The national workshops were created by the provisional government to alleviate the unemployment problem in Paris. They were hated by the rest of the country, though, because of the taxes necessary to fund them. When the workshops were dissolved by the government in June, rebellion broke out in Paris—the so-called "June Days." Option A is incorrect as Louis Philippe had been over-thrown in February. Option B is incorrect as Louis Napoleon's coup did not happen until 1851. Option D is incorrect because it occurred in May.

297. (C) Though both revolutions depended on working-class support, the bour-geoisie only wanted civil liberties and a voice for itself in the government, which could be satisfied be granting suffrage to people with property. When these were granted, the bourgeoisie abandoned the workers and refused to support their demands. Option A is incorrect as both revolutions led to monarchies, and these were often popularly supported. Option B is incorrect as the Catholic Church often reclaimed previously eliminated rights and privileges after 1848. Option D is incorrect as no noble property was confiscated.

298. (D) All Frenchmen would consider themselves patriotic and this was never in question. Since the other options were considered and debated by various revolu-tionary figures, these options are incorrect. Eventually, a dictatorship under Louis Napoleon was created.

299. (A) John Stuart Mill is credited with popularizing laissez-faire economics in his book *The Principles of Political Economy*. This philosophy is the belief that the best thing a government can do for business is to not interfere. Option B is incor-rect as it is Richard Arkwright who is credited with developing the standard factory that became commonplace during the Industrial Revolution. Option C is incorrect as the modern idea of Utopian Socialism is usually attributed to reformers and philosophers such as Robert Owen and Charles Fourier. Option D is incorrect as central planning is opposed to John Stuart Mill's ideas of laissez-faire economics.

300. (A) Although the uprising in Austria and Hungary was suppressed with the aid of Russian troops, laws passed in 1848 led to the abolition of serfdom.

301. (D) The antagonism between the classes under the old order was key to Karl Marx's philosophy. Option A is incorrect because Locke made many statements supporting the protection of private property, which contradicts the Marxist view of property being held by the state for the good of all. Option B is incorrect as

Rousseau never discussed details of class antagonisms or made predictions of future societies. Option C is incorrect because Burke was a conservative and would never say such a quote.

302. (A) Pierre Joseph Proudhon (1809–1865) declared himself anarchist and is considered by some to be the father of the philosophy of anarchism. He is best known for the assertion that anarchy is order without power. (Despite his philosophy of anarchism, later in life he served as a member of the French Parliament.) Options B and D are incorrect. Peter Kropotkin (1842–1921) and Élisée Reclus (1830–1905) were also well-known anarchy theorists, but their lives and careers were subsequent to Proudhon's. Option C is incorrect as Charles Fourier was a well-known proponent of Utopian Socialism.

303. (A) Social Darwinism is the theory, derived from biological Darwinism, that groups and individuals compete against each other and the strongest and most fit survive. This was eventually taken to include racial groups. Option B is incorrect because Marxism was an economic and political theory that ascribed racial and national conflict as illegitimate and masking class struggle. Options C and D are incorrect because they represent philosophies concerned with either the point of existence or how to perceive sensory experiences.

304. (D) The goal of Metternich's Concert of Europe was to preserve peace, the social order, and national boundaries as drawn up at the Congress of Vienna, unless the parties agreed to the change. While there were wars in the 18th century in Europe, the only conflict to take place between member countries that resulted in the forced transfer of territory within Europe was the Franco-Prussian War. It shattered the ideal of peace and stability within Europe and inaugurated the new German nation, which would threaten European stability for 80 years. This would dramatically change the balance of power in Europe. Option A is incorrect because though the Crimean War was between member countries of the Concert of Europe, no major land swaps between them occurred. It did not substantially change the balance of power. Option C presumably refers to the war of Denmark against Prussia and Austria. It resulted in minor transfers of territory and did not greatly change things.

305. (D) The Austrian chancellor Metternich led the Congress of Vienna, which created a system of stability for Europe after the Napoleonic Wars. Metternich's goals were stability and the maintenance of a conservative status quo. The system that was set up followed Metternich's goals for Europe. Options A and C are incorrect because while these were figures who were present, they were not as dominant as Metternich. Option B is incorrect because the entire conference was composed of representatives of countries that had defeated Napoleon I, and he was in exile.

306. (A) Upon inheriting the throne from his brother, Alexander I, Nicholas I put down the Decembrist Revolt of officers in the Russian military in 1825. It was the first manifestation of a modern revolutionary movement in Russia as well as the first and only military-led uprising against civilian authority in that country's history. As a result of the Decembrist Revolt, the leaders were either executed or exiled to Siberia, and Nicholas I strengthened autocratic rule in Russia.

307. (D) After Napoleon's defeat at Waterloo in 1815, he demanded political asylum in Great Britain. However, the decision was made to send him into exile on the island of St. Helena, far from the European mainland.

308. (A) 1871 was the year of the unification of Germany. Before that time, Germany consisted of a collection of independent states that shared not much more than a common language. Under the direction of Otto von Bismarck, Prussia dominated the independent German states, and it united them in a common purpose by engineering a Franco-Prussian War. For the first time in history, men from every other German state joined Prussia and fought united against the French enemy. Option B is incorrect as the Bourbon dynasty was restored after Napoleon was defeated in 1814. Option C is also incorrect. In 1815 the Netherlands and Belgium were joined in order to create a stronger defense against France, but that alliance did not last long. The Quadruple Alliance was formed in 1813 when the four great powers of Europe joined together to defeat France. After France's defeat, the Quadruple Alliance treaty was signed by the members of the alliance in Paris in 1815.

309. (D) Austrian Foreign Minister Klemens von Metternich, along with British Foreign Secretary Lord Castlereagh, primarily feared growing expansion and influence in European affairs, but Metternich also worried about a stronger and bigger Prussia. Czar Alexander I of Russia wanted to undo the partitions of Poland and bring that country under Russian control. To do that he would need the permission of Prussia. Prussia agreed, if Russia would support its claim to the entire Kingdom of Saxony. News of a secret pact between France, Britain, and Austria to go to war against Prussia and Russia if necessary over the Polish-Saxon question led Alexander I to back down and compromise, accepting a reduced Poland called "Congress Poland," and Prussia received two-fifths of Saxony while the rest remained to the Saxon king.

310. (D) Metternich led the way in trying to organize collective security arrangements with the leading powers of Europe to stamp out any manifestations of revolutionary challenges to the post–Congress of Vienna order. His closest allies became Russia and Prussia, with France occasionally on board and Britain rarely wanting to commit itself to collective security agreements on the continent.

311. (A) Initially Britain was willing to counter any resurgence of French expansionism on the continent but reserved the right to act independently according to its own national interests—not bound by collective security agreements.

For example, the British refused to entertain the proposal of an international naval organization that would combat the slave trade and the Barbary pirates. The British also rejected the principles of collective security devised by Metternich at the Congress of Troppau.

312. (D) The general theme of Metternich's congresses, starting from the Congress of Vienna, was to create a system of reliable order and stability in Europe. Each of these succeeding congresses aimed to do just that. Option A is incorrect as the congresses made no demands on how its participants ran their respective governments, and many of the participating nations were tyrannies of one sort or another. Option B is incorrect as France was admitted as a full member at Aix-la-Chapelle and did not have to make regular payments. Option C is incorrect as this was mostly done at the Congress of Vienna.

313. (D) Liverpool, which began as a fishing village, built its first port in 1715. It added four more ports in the 18th century and became the country's leading city for cotton cloth production as well as a major slave-trading hub. In the 19th century, it expanded its docks even more and built a shipping canal to Manchester to facilitate trade with that city. By the end of the 19th century, it had become the largest port in the country outside of London. Both Birmingham (Option A) and Manchester (Option B) were major English industrial cities, but both cities were landlocked. After building a canal to allow ships to come to the city, Manchester did become a major port, but it was never as busy as Liverpool. Option C is incorrect as Oxford was a center of education and learning and not a city with an industrial sector.

314. (C) The Decembrist Revolt was a rebellion of Russian officers demanding more constitutional rights and modernization from the government. Nicholas I ruthlessly cracked down on them. Options A and B have nothing to do with Russia and did not occur in 1825. Option D occurred in 1861.

315. (B) The Austrian Empire gave way to the dual monarchy of Austria-Hungary, midcentury. It was a way to preserve the peace between the two largest components of the Austrian Empire. Hungarian nobles agreed to the compromise that created the Austro-Hungarian Empire. Option A is incorrect because it never existed; they were both united in the new German nation. Option C is incorrect because it only existed as the United Kingdom of the Netherlands for 15 years, until the Belgian rebellion of 1830. Option D is incorrect because Poland had a king that operated under the Russian emperor, until Poland was completely absorbed by Russia in 1830.

316. (C) This term was created by Johann Herder, who suggested that each nation had its own nature and national talents. Options A and B are both incorrect as while Volksgeist could lead to unification movements, it does not refer to specific German or Italian unification movements. Option D is incorrect as the term has nothing to do with war reparations.

317. (C) The Frankfurt Parliament of 1848 was an attempt to create a constitution for a united Germany, with a kaiser as a constitutional monarch. It failed and was crushed by Austria and Prussia. Option A is incorrect because it was a response to revolutionary events in Europe in 1848, not Prussia. Option B is incorrect because the Zollverein was created many years before. Option D is incorrect because the Frankfort Parliament was a way to create a united German state, not a confederation of cities.

318. (B) Bismarck came from a Junker family. Junkers were Prussian nobles.

319. (A) All other choices had greater reason to fear a united Prussian-dominated Germany than Russia. Option B is incorrect as Prussia was Austria's greatest rival. Option C is incorrect because Hanover was forcibly annexed by Prussia as part of German unification. Option D is incorrect because of Danish hatred of Germany following their loss in the Wars of Schleswig.

320. (C) The Ottoman Empire had been in decline for centuries before it finally collapsed after World War I. However, much European diplomacy had to do with whether to hasten that decline or to try to stop it. Austria-Hungary and the United Kingdom sought to preserve it, whereas other powers sought to speed its demise. Option A is incorrect because Austria was not considered eastern. Option B is incorrect as the Russian Empire was not in decline yet. Option D is incorrect because it is certainly in the east, but not in the eastern end of Europe.

321. (B) The Decembrist Revolt took place in 1825, at the beginning of the reign of Nicholas I. The rebellious officers were trying to have Constantine, the brother of dead Czar Alexander, become czar instead of the rightful heir, Nicholas. They failed. The other options represent czars that ruled at other times.

322. (D) In 1830, because of Charles X's enforcement of repressive ordinances, a rebellion sprang up in France. The result of the rebellion was the abdication of Charles X and the declaration that Louis-Philippe was "king of the French by the grace of God and the will of the people." Option A is incorrect as this vote in 1825 was one of the reasons the revolution began. (In 1825 the legislative chambers voted to compensate émigrés who lost land in the first French Revolution "perpetually," totaling 30 million francs a year.) Option B is also incorrect. The Congress of Vienna did not impose a crushing burden of government reparations on France. Option C is incorrect as Louis Napoleon Bonaparte was not elected president until 1848.

323. (B) The British parliament enacted the Reform Act of 1832 after a contentious public debate lasting several years and it embraced electoral reforms, expanding representation in Parliament to include emerging major cities. It also expanded the vote to many in the middle classes, although not to the working class, so (C) is incorrect.

324. (C) Belgium was the only country to undergo a successful revolution and independence when Catholics in the southern part of the country led an uprising against the Dutch who ruled Belgium at the time.

325. (B) Louis Philippe had Republican sympathies during the French Revolution, but was also a Bourbon, though more removed from the line of succession than Charles X. He was therefore acceptable to Republicans, Liberals, and Royalists. Option A is incorrect as Louis Philippe never had that position. Option C is incorrect because Louis Philippe had actually been friendly with Charles X in the years leading up to 1830 and had even been acting as regent for the grandson that Charles hoped would succeed him. Option D is incorrect as Louis Philippe had never fought in America.

326. (C) The Industrial Revolution became entrenched in France by 1848, and with it, Socialist ideas. Many of the leaders of the rebellion were Socialists, though the Revolution of 1848 did not produce a Socialist government. Option A is incorrect because though 3,000 were killed, that number is less than other rebellions in 1830 and 1848 and is not particularly unique. Option B is incorrect as it never happened. Option D is incorrect because this occurred many times before and after 1848.

327. (C) Karl Marx did extensive writing about the Revolution of 1848 in France, such as *The Eighteenth Brumaire of Louis Napoleon*. Options A, B, and D refer to people who died before 1848.

328. (B) Kaiser Wilhelm, the eldest grandchild of Queen Victoria, was king of Prussia. A military man, he waged war on Denmark, Austria, and France. During the war with France, he proclaimed himself emperor (Kaiser) of Germany, which he had united during the wars. Option A is incorrect, although Bismarck is the man who helped create the North German Confederation from disparate nations. Options C and D are incorrect as neither of these men ruled Germany. Louis Philippe was a French ruler, while Nicholas I was a Russian monarch.

329. (C) France lost the Franco-Prussian War in 1870, and Louis Napoleon was captured by the Germans. He was officially deposed, and the French Third Republic was born. He spent the rest of his life in England. Options A and B are incorrect as they occurred a number of years before this. Option D, the Dreyfus Affair, occurred more than 20 years after Louis Napoleon was captured by the Germans and deposed.

330. (C) Bismarck saw that adult male suffrage would lead to peasants outvoting urban workers. Bismarck was most afraid of Socialists and saw this as a strategic way to block their election. Option A is incorrect because Bismarck was at heart a conservative man. Option B is incorrect because all men did not have the right to vote in England at this time. Option D is incorrect because the emperor said no such thing, nor would anybody expect him to.

331. (B) It was a policy of Russia since the times of Peter the Great to gain more influence in the Ottoman Empire through the Christian Orthodox population (Greeks, Serbs, Bulgarians, Romanians, and Slavic Macedonians). By failing to support Alexander Ypsilanti's Greek uprising against Ottoman rule in 1821, Alexander I chose instead to support Metternich's policy of defense against revolutionary uprisings.

332. (B) The Congress of Troppau was formed to deal with revolutionaries in Naples and other places. Britain and France (to a lesser degree) objected to intervention by other European powers in the Naples revolution. The division caused by this Congress severely weakened the Quintuple Alliance. Option A is incorrect as the result of the Congress of Aix-la-Chapelle was to end the occupation of France by the allies and to admit France as a member of the then-renamed Quintuple Alliance. Option C is incorrect. The Congress of Verona was called in part to deal with the Spanish question, and permission was eventually given—over British objections—to the French to return Ferdinand VII to the Spanish throne. Option D is also incorrect. The July Ordinances were a set of decrees that Charles X published. They dealt with the internal matters of France.

333. (B) In 1876, Serbia declared war on the Ottoman Empire and proclaimed unification with Bosnia, whose population was predominantly Slavic and Christian Orthodox. Serbian expectations were that Bosnia would be united with Serbia proper, but instead, the leading powers at the Treaty of Berlin decided to cede it to Austria-Hungary. Option A is incorrect as Croatia's population, although linguistically and racially related to the Serbs, was Catholic and already part of the Austro-Hungarian Empire. Option C is incorrect as Kosovo remained part of the Ottoman Empire until 1913, when it was reunited with Serbia. Option D is incorrect as Slovenia had a negligible Serbian population and had already been part of the Austro-Hungarian Empire.

334. (D) Russian Czar Nicholas I intended to send troops to crush the Belgian uprising against Dutch rule in 1830 but was distracted by an uprising in Poland against Russian rule. Neither the British nor French came to the support of the Poles, who were defeated by the Russians. Congress Poland was abolished along with its constitution and fully incorporated into the Russian Empire. Meanwhile, events in Belgium led to its independence in 1831, agreed upon by France and Great Britain. It had become too late for Russia to intervene.

335. (A) Revolutions in France and Belgium sparked an uprising in Poland against Russian rule. This uprising failed when Czar Nicholas I sent troops to crush the rebellion. Congress Poland was abolished along with its constitution and fully incorporated into the Russian Empire. The Polish Catholic Church was allowed to operate. Ukraine and Belarus had been reincorporated into Russia during the partitions of Poland in the 18th century, long before the 1830 uprising.

336. (C) Nationalism posed a major challenge to the unity of the Ottoman Empire as the Serbs and Greeks were the first among the Christian Europeans to fight for their independence from the Muslim Turks. The same nationalist challenges to the Austrian Empire were felt as the non-German populations in that country (Magyars, Romanians, Czechs, Slovaks, Serbs, Croatians, and Slovenes) demanded more political autonomy. The Poles challenged Russian rule twice in the 19th century, until they finally gained their independence in 1918. Option A is incorrect because although German unification was motivated by nationalist ideas, Germany was largely a unitary state, overwhelmingly dominated by ethnic Germans, with only about 5 percent of the population ethnically Polish. Italian unification was the unification of ethnically Italian states. Option B is incorrect as the growth of nationalism did not lead to an overall strengthening of the Catholic Church in Europe. Finally, Option D is incorrect because although the multi-ethnic states fought on opposite sides in World War I, this happened in the 20th century, not the 19th.

337. (B) The Treaty of San Stefano in 1878 was a peace treaty imposed on the Ottoman Empire by Russia after Russia's victory in the Russo-Turkish war. The treaty granted Romania, Serbia, and Bulgaria independence. Option A is incorrect, although Russia was the country that facilitated their independence from the Ottoman Empire. Options C and D are incorrect as well, as neither Austria-Hungary or Greece had conquered these countries.

338. (C) The Congress of Verona was called in part to deal with the Spanish question, and permission was eventually given, over British objections, to the French to return Ferdinand VII to the Spanish throne. Option A is incorrect as the result of the Congress of Aix-la-Chapelle was to end the occupation of France by the allies, and to admit France as a member of the now renamed Quintuple Alliance. Option B is incorrect as the result of the Congress of Troppau was to deal with revolutionaries in Naples and other places. Option D is incorrect as the Congress of Vienna was convened to deal with the situation in Europe immediately after the fall of Napoleon.

339. (C) During 1830, Poland erupted in rebellion against Russia. While Russia, Prussia, and Austria would have liked to have seen the Belgian rebellion put down, they were too focused on crushing the Polish rebellion. Therefore, they went along with the British and French policy of noninterference.

340. (A) Rasputin was a mystic with close connections to Czar Nicholas II and his family, a relationship many Russians considered unhealthy. Samsonov was a general in charge of Russian troops during World War I, Trotsky was an influential Marxist theorist, and Turgenev was a well regarded Russian novelist.

341. (D) Nationalists believed in the importance and unique characteristics of different nationalities and that they should be respected and allowed to flourish, usually in their national homelands. All other choices contradict this ideal or have nothing to do with it. Option A is incorrect as nationalists may or may not believe in human rights. Options B and C are incorrect as nationalism officially has nothing to do with Socialism, free trade, or economics in general.

342. (D) Nationalists traditionally valued the unique traits of their nations and often had idealized visions of their countries. A romanticized national ideal was often at the heart of their movements. It is hard to ascribe ideological aspects to the early nationalist movements. Therefore, all other options, which do have political, economic, or social agendas, cannot accurately characterize nationalism of the period.

343. (B) The purpose of the Congress of Aix-la-Chapelle was to end the occupation of France by the allies and to admit France as a member of the now-renamed Quintuple Alliance. Options A and B are incorrect. The Alliance had formerly been known as the Quadruple Alliance and had been formed by the United Kingdom, Austria, Prussia, and Russia to counter the aggression of France. Option C is also incorrect as Italy was never a part of that alliance.

344. (B) Russia had intervened, along with Britain and France, in the cause of Greek independence in 1821. Options A and C are incorrect as these countries had nothing to do with the war. Option D is incorrect as it was the Ottoman Empire that the Greeks were fighting to free themselves from.

345. (B) The Greek rebellion had substantial support from Britain, France, and Russia, and as such, they insisted that the new government be a monarchy. A Bavarian prince assumed the throne of the newly independent Greece. Option A is incorrect as Socialism was still a very immature idea, supported by few in Western Europe, let alone Greece. Option C is incorrect because it might have been possible but was disallowed by the Great Powers. Option D is incorrect because the revolutionaries wanted a functioning unified country and were more linguistically united than in classical Greece.

346. (B) The rebellion in Greece created a movement called philhellenism, where popular support was aroused in the west for Greek independence, based in part on the view that Greece was the foundation of western civilization. Russians traditionally sympathized with and aided their Christian brethren in the Balkans, like the Greeks, Serbs, and Bulgarians who fought against Muslim Turkish occupation. Option A is incorrect as no such offers were made. Option C is incorrect as he did not study at the Sorbonne, and this would hardly have been enough reason to get involved in a war. Option D is incorrect as there was no famine caused by the Turks.

347. (C) From the late 18th century through the 19th century, Poland was invaded by Russia, Prussia, and Austria, and its land was partitioned off to these powers. Because of this, the country disappeared from the map until 1918. The Great Polish Emigration began in 1831 after a failed uprising and included subsequent waves after uprisings throughout the century. During this time, it was the Polish emigrants who assumed many of the intellectual functions of their nonexistent state. Their displaced enclaves became the centers of literary, artistic, and scientific Polish life as well as political and social growth for the country. Because of the important role these emigrants played in the development of Poland, historians named this the "Great Emigration."

348. (C) The first Zionist Congress was held in 1897, just a year after the publication of Herzl's book. Option A is incorrect as Jews had been immigrating to the United States before the book was published. Option B is incorrect as the Ottoman Empire never declared that Jews could not go to Palestine. Option D is incorrect because Jews from Arab countries did not move to Palestine until after the declaration of the state of Israel in 1948.

349. (D) Pogroms, or organized riots against Jews sponsored by the government, took place in Russia. All other options are incorrect as no such actions occurred there.

350. (B) Most of Prussia's wars resulting in territorial expansion came at the expense of the Austrians. In the Austrian Wars of Succession (1740–1748) and the Seven Years' War (1756–1763), Prussia gained control of all of Silesia. A century later, the Prussians defeated Austria in the Austro-Prussian War (1866) and annexed pro-Austrian German states as well as all of Schleswig-Holstein. Option A is incorrect, although Prussia did take some territory from the French after the Franco-Prussian war. More important to Prussia than land acquisition was that Prussia's victory over the French in 1870 directly led to the creation of the German Empire. Option C is incorrect, although Prussia did win some territory from Denmark after their conflict. Option D is incorrect as Holland did not sacrifice territory.

351. (C) Britain was interested in maintaining good communication and sea routes to India, as well as the prime agricultural land in southern Africa. Accordingly, Britain conquered the majority of southern Africa. Option A is incorrect as the French were more dominant in western Africa. Option B is incorrect as Italy was more active in Ethiopia and Libya. Option D is incorrect as Belgium controlled only the Congo in central Africa.

352. (A) The idea of Social Darwinism is that certain races are superior to others and, therefore, justified in conquering others. As a result the white man should shoulder the burden of teaching a superior culture to the lesser races. Option B is incorrect because those who believe in the "white man's burden" would not respect native traditions. Options C and D are ideologies of the 19th century that would regard racism and cultural superiority as primitive and ignorant.

353. (B) The job of missionaries is to spread religion. Therefore, they tried to do this in Africa as much as possible. Option A is incorrect because missionaries had no slaves. Option C is incorrect as most missionaries had little particular interest in tribal culture. Option D is incorrect as missionaries have no reason to study rivers.

354. (C) Unbridled competition for Africa could lead to war between European powers. The Berlin Conference was set up to establish rules for the conquest and competition for Africa by the Europeans; therefore, Option B is incorrect. Option A is incorrect as Leopold was given the area around the Congo River. Option D is wrong as the participants discussed the whole continent, not just the Congo.

355. (B) The Portuguese constructed ports and trading posts along the coast of Mozambique starting in the 1500s. However, it was only in the late 1800s—after some major battles—that Portugal was able to take control of the country and claim it as a colony. Option A is incorrect as Zimbabwe was colonized by Britain. Option C is also incorrect as Togo was colonized by Germany and later France. Option D is incorrect as King Leopold of Belgium took over the Congo as his almost personal dominion, ruling it with a particularly cruel administration.

356. (C) Because of external debts, the Egyptian leadership sold their shares in the canal to Britain. However, the majority of the shares were still owned by French business interests. Option A is incorrect as Turkey had nothing to do with the creation or operation of the canal. Option D is incorrect because it did not even exist at the time.

357. (C) Although oil had been discovered and produced in large quantities in the United States and Russia prior to 1908, its discovery in Persia in 1908 by the British Anglo-Persian Oil Company opened the way to even more discoveries of petroleum in Iraq, Bahrain, and Saudi Arabia in the period between the World Wars. The increasing popularity of gasoline-powered cars created a growing demand for oil that continues to this day, making the Middle East much more important than ever before.

358. (C) These areas were conquered and added to the Russian Empire in the first half of the century. Option A is incorrect as Russia has never had a presence in the Pacific Islands. Option B is incorrect because though Russia held northwestern North America for a time, it never got close to South America. Option D is incorrect as the Russian Empire never got farther south than Central Asia.

359. (D) The Suez Canal connects the Mediterranean Sea to the Red Sea by creating a shipping channel between the Sinai Peninsula and Africa. Therefore, ships did not have to go around all of Africa to go from Europe to the Indian Ocean.

Option A is incorrect as it applies to the Panama Canal, which bisects the Panamanian isthmus at its narrowest point. Option B is incorrect because while there are oil refineries adjacent to the canal, they are not of particular strategic importance and were not the main reason for the canal's construction. Option C is incorrect because revenue from the canal goes to the Egyptian government.

360. (A) Britain practiced a policy called "divide and rule," which took advantage of Muslim-Hindu tensions. It may have led to the eventual partition of India and Pakistan. Option B is incorrect because the Portuguese had been driven out of India long before the British were able to establish control over it. Option C is incorrect because no Mughals had invited anyone from the outside into India. Option D is incorrect as British consumer goods were not greatly available in the mid–19th century. This is in addition to the majority of Indians having no ability to pay for such things at the time.

361. (B) The British East India Company had actually ruled India, not the British government itself. The British government took over India directly after 1857. Option A is incorrect because the Mughal Empire had already declined before British rule came to India. Option C is incorrect because the sepoys, or Indian soldiers working for the British, had been trained after the British East India Company arrived and controlled India. Option D is incorrect because the British East India Company had conquered India initially.

362. (B) There was resentment and rumors among Indians about efforts, real or imagined, to convert Indians to Anglican Christianity. This was made worse by the tallow controversy, when Indian sepoy troops thought they were being ordered to tear open with their mouths gun cartridges made with cow or pig tallow—offensive to both Hindus and Muslims. Option A is incorrect as there was no salt monopoly. Option C is incorrect because there were no French in India at the time. Option D is incorrect because mass violence began with the sepoys.

363. (B) When the Sepoy Rebellion was over, the British government decided that the British East India Company had mismanaged India and assumed direct control over British India. Option A is incorrect because India became a British territory, not a protectorate. Option C is incorrect because it was the end of the British East India Company, not the beginning. Option D is incorrect because though there was some military reorganization, after the rebellion, Indians continued to be used by the British army.

364. (D) Though a small, educated middle class emerged in British India, the living conditions for the majority of Indians declined. The reasons for this are debated by historians. Option A is incorrect as a new class of educated Indian elites began to grow. Option B is incorrect as the British tried to eliminate archaic Indian practices. Option C is incorrect as the British built roads and railroads in India.

365. (A) There was a great sphere of domestic industry that existed in India prior to the arrival of the British. This was greatly destroyed by a classic imperialist economic policy that required India to become a market for British manufactured goods. Option B is incorrect as British India became less economically advanced as time went on. Option C is incorrect because any technological improvements to India were done to allow more British economic exploitation. Option D is incorrect because taxes were actually lower during this time than during the Mogul Empire.

366. (C) British India continued to export agricultural products, including foodstuffs, during famines. This was a direct result of British policies encouraging these exports to other countries such as China as payment for other goods. Option A is incorrect as Indian farmers did worse economically under the British. Option B is incorrect as Indian agriculture continued to be backward. Option D is incorrect as Britain continued its economic decline relative to Germany and the United States.

367. (B) The Opium War was humiliating for the Chinese, and they finally realized how far behind the West they had fallen. Option A is incorrect because there were no opium-caused famines. Option C is incorrect as Portugal was never a major player in China. Option D is incorrect because there was no way for China to use opium against the British.

368. (B) Hong Kong became a British colony for the next 99 years. This was a major embarrassment for the Chinese until the lease ran out. Option A did not occur. Option C did not occur as China continued to have a classic, though distinctly unmodern navy, which was no threat to Britain. Option D is wrong because it would just hurt locals more than it would help China.

369. (B) The Taiping Rebellion was an internal rebellion sponsored by a religious cult called the God Worshipping Society. It was fought over economic conditions and lasted from 1850 to 1864. It led to the deaths of more than 20 million people. In order to finally subdue the rebellion, imperial forces in China began using soldiers provided by Britain and France. They also hired mercenaries, the most famous in that conflict being the American Frederick Ward. Option A is incorrect as the Boxer Rebellion did not result in the deaths of millions of people, and it was fought in 1900. However, the Boxer Rebellion did weaken the Chinese government. The Boxers were particularly interested in freeing China from foreigners. To that end, Christian missionaries were often attacked as representatives of what some Chinese considered a totally alien religion. When the Boxers were defeated, China had to pay reparations to the foreign countries who had come in to subdue the rebellion. Options C and D are incorrect as the Communist Revolution did not happen until 1948 and the Cultural Revolution did not happen until the 1960s.

370. (C) The Germans were alarmed at what they saw as the rapid modernization of their eastern neighbor and thought it was just a matter of time before Russia eclipsed Germany as the most advanced economy in Europe. Therefore, they felt war was inevitable and that it would be better for the Germans if it came sooner rather than later. Option A is incorrect because Russia and Austria were rivals, not allies. Option B is incorrect because the Russian fleet was nowhere near the size of the German fleet. Option D is incorrect because no militarization of the border had gone on, and officially there was no German-Polish border, as Poland was mostly within the Russian Empire.

371. (C) There was no alliance between Germany and Russia at this time. Russia was allied with Britain and France. Option A is incorrect because it is true that Germany had dreams of creating a navy to match Britain's. Option B is incorrect because there were colonial rivalries among all the powers of Europe. Option D is incorrect because there was increasing German involvement in the Balkans, particularly the proposed rail link between Germany and Baghdad.

372. (B) "Our nation" in the passage refers to Germany. It arrived late to the game of imperialism and had to take the less desirable of colonies, but this passage shows the attitude of Germany in the late 19th-century to early 20th-century period of wanting to surpass more established European powers. Option A is incorrect as Russia had no plans or ability to create overseas imperialism as it had an enormous empire that was connected to it. Options C and D are incorrect because both had already created enormous overseas empires.

373. (A) With the creation of a new independent Bulgaria, and the coming to power of Serbian nationalists in Serbia, the Austro-Hungarians were afraid of a new power to their south. They, therefore, preemptively annexed Bosnia-Herzegovina in 1908 and almost started a major war. Option B is incorrect because Austria-Hungary had a rivalry, not an alliance with Russia. Option C is incorrect because Austria-Hungary was not an ally of Britain. Option D is incorrect because the Austro-Hungarians feared Slavs and would not want another Slav state on their borders.

374. (C) Gibraltar continues to be a British possession. Consisting of six square kilometers, it is considered a strategic position as it guards to entrance to the Mediterranean Sea. The British captured the land from Spain in 1704, and since then it has been ceded to Britain "in perpetuity" through a number of treaties. Most of the citizens of Gibraltar have no wish to be granted independence. Options A, B, and D are all incorrect. Egypt was granted independence in 1922, Malta was granted independence in 1964, and Cyprus was granted independence in 1960.

375. (C) It was fear of Russian expansion southward into the Balkans that kept Britain and France involved in the reinforcement of the declining Ottoman Empire in the 19th century, even going so far as to fight Russia in the Crimean War. Russia was seen as the main threat to the Balkans and Mediterranean until later, when the threat of Germany became much greater. Option A is incorrect because while Britain was becoming more religiously tolerant, this had nothing to do with diplomacy in the Balkans or Asia Minor. Option B is incorrect because if anything the British sympathized with the Greeks. Option D is incorrect because personal regard for individual leaders had very little to do with diplomacy during this period.

376. (A) Louis David was the only artist listed not part of the Romantic movement. He was of the French neoclassical style and is famous for his portraits of the leaders and martyrs of the French Revolution. He later was appointed as an official painter for Napoleon Bonaparte's court

377. (C) The importance of the subconscious was first emphasized by Sigmund Freud, the pioneering psychoanalyst. It is in the field of social science. Romanticism is generally an artistic movement. Option A is incorrect because moods and expressions are at the center of Romanticism. Option B is incorrect because customs that cannot be classified or analyzed describe behaviors based on unscientific feelings and moods, the hallmark of Romanticism. Nationalism, the subject of many Romantic paintings and other works of art, is often based on the peculiar customs of national identity. Option D is incorrect as Romantics saw emotion at the very center of what they were trying to appeal to.

378. (A) Jacques-Louis David was a painter of the neoclassical style, which preceded Romanticism. He is famous for paintings such as *The Death of Marat*. Eugene Delacroix, Option B, was a leader of the French Romantic school of painting. Lord Byron, Option C, was an English Romantic poet. Option D, Victor Hugo, was a French Romantic writer of books such as *Les Misérables*.

379. (B) Alexander Pope was a noted English satirical writer and poet of the early 18th century, prior to the Romantic period. William Wordsworth (A) and Samuel Taylor Coleridge (C) are considered founding fathers of English Romantic poetry, while William Blake (D) was not as well recognized during his lifetime but is now considered one of the key creators in the Romantic Age.

380. (C) Sir Walter Scott is credited with creating the historical novel. His first novel, *Waverley*, conjured up life in the Scottish Highlands in the mid-1700s. Hollywood would later adapt some of his books to the big screen. Option B is incorrect. Although Austen is regarded as one of the greatest novelists in the English language, her books dealt with the social mores of the British upper classes in the late 18th and early 19th centuries. Option A is incorrect as Goethe is considered the preeminent writer of the German literary canon; while his works are rooted in Romanticism, his work is usually described as classical, spanning several artistic eras from the Enlightenment forward. Option D is incorrect as Victor Hugo is one of the major voices of the French Romantic literary arena.

381. (B) Nationalists were frequently conservatives who harkened back to an idealized time of order and national purity. Conservatives could appeal to the more negative side of nationalism, that which saw anything foreign as evil and distrusted anything alien. Options A and D are incorrect as Socialists and radicals often saw themselves through the lens of class-consciousness, which transcends national borders. Option C is incorrect as liberals were more interested in practical reforms of society, not romanticized notions of nationhood.

Period 4

382. (A) The chain of events that led to World War I started when a Serbian man assassinated Archduke Ferdinand of Austria-Hungary. When Serbia refused to abide by the ultimatum quoted in the question, Austria-Hungary declared war on Serbia, and other countries took sides and declared war on countries of enemy alliances. All other options are incorrect because though they took part in the war, they issued no ultimatums, but simply followed alliance obligations.

383. (C) Prior to the annexation, 42 percent of Bosnia's population was Orthodox Serbian, 40 percent was Muslim, and 18 percent was Catholic Croat. Naturally, Serbs in Serbia felt that Bosnia should eventually become part of a greater independent Serbian state and, therefore, Austria's annexation caused deep hostility among Serbian nationalists toward Austria. Option A is incorrect as the Ottoman leadership had several separatist movements to deal with and realized that it would be fruitless to challenge Austria over Bosnia. Option B is incorrect as Romania had no ethnic affinities with the Bosnian population. Option D is incorrect as Bulgarians never had a legitimate territorial claim on Bosnia.

384. (C) Bolshevism became a serious force during the Russian Revolution, but was of little significance before it and had no impact on the causes of World War I. Option A is incorrect as historians believe the alliance system was a clear cause of the chain reaction that started the war. Option B is incorrect because there was a clear armaments competition between the combatants, helped by the greed of arms manufacturers. Option D is incorrect because Balkan nationalism caused the assassination that triggered the war in 1914.

385. (D) Germany and Austria-Hungary were competitors during the German unification process, and Bismarck arranged for Germany to grow at Austria-Hungary's expense. However, common interests led to an alliance during World War I. Option A is incorrect as France and Russia allied with each other in the years preceding World War I. Option B is incorrect as Serbia and Russia were natural allies and their alliance before and during the war helped create the war in the first place. Option C is incorrect because Great Britain and Belgium were not allied but became allied when Germany disregarded Belgium's neutral status and attacked.

386. (C) The Schlieffen Plan anticipated Germany being squeezed between France and Russia. Therefore, it called for France to be knocked out of the war early, so that Germany could concentrate on Russia. Option A is incorrect as Germany knew Russia would be in the war and fully planned on how to deal with it. Option B is incorrect as Germany believed the key to success lay in knocking France out quickly and fully believed this could be done. Option D is incorrect as Austria-Hungary, plus Italy, and the Ottoman Empire were to the south of Germany and would not prevent Germany from fighting a two-front war in any case.

387. (B) The Triple Alliance refers to the Central Powers of World War I, which consisted of Germany, Austria-Hungary, and Italy. Option A is incorrect because Russia joined it to oppose the Triple Alliance. Option C refers to an alliance created earlier that included Germany, Austria-Hungary, and Russia. Option D is incorrect because it refers to the winning alliance of World War II, of which Russia was a member.

388. (C) France and Germany almost came to war because of the two crises over Morocco. The first took place in 1905, and the second took place in 1911. Germany wanted to have access to the Moroccan ports and the Moroccan market, which France had almost exclusive control of. Option A is incorrect because England and France had just signed an alliance treaty at the beginning of the 20th century. Option B is incorrect because Morocco was a weak independent country that was quickly being colonized by both England and France. Option D is incorrect because Italy had almost no interest in Morocco at that time.

389. (B) The greatest naval power in the world at the outset of World War I was Great Britain. With the aid of its navy, the British were able to create a global empire. Since 1898 Germany's naval program had grown, and by 1912 it became a threat to the British. Option D is incorrect because the United States had been growing its navy, but it could not compare to that of Great Britain yet. Options A and C are incorrect because although they were substantial European powers, they did not have navies that could compare with that of Britain's. Therefore the British did not see them as threats.

390. (B) Most of World War I in the western front was fought in northeastern France, where trench warfare had been established after the initial stages of the war. Option A is incorrect as the Germans had entrenched themselves in France at the beginning of the war after going through Belgium. Option C is incorrect as Britain was separated from the main theater of war by water. Option D is incorrect as the Netherlands was never in the war.

391. (C) There were parades, cheering, and a great deal of popular enthusiasm for the war at its beginning in Germany, Austria, Russia, and other countries. Most believed victory would occur in a matter of weeks. The reality was sobering. All other options are opposite to the tone of great support for the war.

392. (D) Britain adopted conscription in World War I, the last country to do so. All other options are incorrect because they happened earlier, starting with France during the French Revolution.

393. (D) Defensive weapons and tactics such as machine guns and trenches without an improvement in offensive weapons and tactics led to the stalemate of the World War I trenches. It was not until the advent of tanks and accurate aerial bombing that this situation could be changed. Option A is incorrect as airplanes had a mostly minor role in World War I since their bombing was quite inaccurate. Option B is incorrect because snipers were insignificant next to mines, gas, and machine guns. Option C is inaccurate because the fighting took place on plains, which were fine for assembling large armies.

394. (D) It would be absurd to use cavalry to overcome trench warfare. The horses would immediately be mowed down by machine guns, along with their riders. The technology of Option A was used toward the end of the war but was not completely effective as the tanks were primitive and the troops were just beginning to learn how to use them. They would be instrumental in making trench warfare obsolete in World War II. Other options are incorrect because they were actually used and were ineffective.

395. (C) The atrocities in Belgium stirred up outrage in Britain at the beginning of the war when Germany invaded France through Belgium. The other options are incorrect because they are events that occurred later than the start of the war.

396. (D) England was the last country in the list to enter World War I. It entered the war when Germany refused to withdraw from Belgium, after Germany had invaded that country to get to France. Option C is incorrect because the war started when a Serbian nationalist assassinated the Austrian archduke and Austria-Hungary declared war on Serbia. Option A is incorrect because Russia declared war on Austria-Hungary to support Serbia. Option B is incorrect because the French were allied with Russia.

397. (B) Italy entered into the war in 1915 on the side of Britain, France, and the Russian Empire. Italy argued that its participation in the Triple Alliance was defensive in nature and it did not have to take part in the war on the side of Germany and Austria-Hungary. Option A is incorrect because Italy had entered on the side of the Entente Powers in 1915 and not on the side of the Central Powers. Option C is incorrect because Italy decided to enter the war in 1915 and not stay neutral. Option D is incorrect because the United States did not enter the war until 1917, two years after Italy entered the war.

398. (D) In order to prevent the Ottoman Empire (Turkey) from controlling the Middle East and the Suez Canal link to India, the British helped the Arabs who were fighting the Ottomans. Option A is incorrect as the British did not necessarily want to see these lands become independent and did not come through with promises that the Arabs thought had been made by the British to create a new independent Arab homeland. Option B is incorrect as the issue of a Jewish state was not addressed until 1917 and was not a concern for most of the war. Option C is incorrect as there was minimal French and Russian influence at the time.

399. (D) Wilson's Fourteen Points called for the creation of new nations, an organization for resolving international disputes, and lenient terms toward Germany. The treaty was much more punitive, and included severe reparations and punishment of Germany in particular. Option A is incorrect because, while true, it was not a fundamental difference between them. Option B is incorrect because the Allies did have some governmental restraints on their own diplomacy. Option C is incorrect because if anything, Wilson was more supporting of a League of Nations.

400. (D) France after World War I sought to remove Germany as a threat. Accordingly, France made sure that the treaty oversight contained provisions that were intended to limit the strength of Germany. This would prevent Germany from attacking France in the future, or so it was hoped. Option A is incorrect because while the French sought revenge against Germany, most French thinking was directed toward future German aggression and preventing it. Option B is incorrect because the French were in no mood to forgive the Germans after World War I and made sure that the Germans paid reparations after the war. Option C is incorrect because the French were clearly not indifferent to Germany and sought reparations and punishment for Germany after the war.

401. (C) None of Wilson's Fourteen Points made any reference to Africa. He was mostly concerned with issues in Europe and the causes of the war in the first place. Option A is incorrect because national self-determination was a cornerstone of the Fourteen Points and was considered to be essential to ending the ethnic question in Europe. Option B is incorrect because Wilson believed the creation of the League of Nations would prevent future wars. Option D is incorrect because Wilson believed that peace without reparations would be a way to declare that the war was not the fault of any one particular nation and would prevent future grudges from being created.

402. (D) The quoted action is the so-called "war-guilt clause" that Germany was forced to sign. It was used to justify the huge reparations that Germany was forced to pay after the war. Option A is incorrect as the League of Nations had no power to impose sanctions of any kind. Option B is incorrect as no disarmament took place other than in Germany. Option C is incorrect as Germany was excluded from the peace negotiations until the end when it was presented as a fait accompli.

403. (D) The League of Nations designated Palestine, Syria, Lebanon, Jordan, and Iraq to become "mandates" of the British and French, which meant the two European powers divided and administered them. Prior to the end of World War I, these territories were part of the Ottoman Empire. Option A is incorrect because they had military forces in them. Option B is incorrect because they were directly administered by outsiders, without much local autonomy. Option C is incorrect because a mandate is a political not an economic term.

404. (A) The Sykes-Picot Agreement was created after World War I to carve up the Middle Eastern territories of the Ottoman Empire between Britain and France. Option B is incorrect as this was a peace process developed between Israel and the Palestinians in 1991. Option C is incorrect as this was a statement of support for a Jewish homeland in Israel by the British in 1917. Option D is incorrect as this refers to a short-term agreement on Arab-Jewish cooperation in the Middle East in 1919.

405. (C) A mandate was supposed to be a transitional period of administering a nation until it was ready for independence. Option A is incorrect as mandates applied to colonies whether or not they were German. Option B is incorrect as a country administering the mandate worked by itself without involving the elites of the society and there was no set time period. Option D is incorrect because indigenous cultures were not considered.

406. (A) The Balfour Declaration of 1917 was the official statement of support for Jewish emigration to British Mandate Palestine and the establishment of a Jewish homeland there. Option B is incorrect as Israel and Jordan did not exist. Option C is incorrect because that announcement would not happen until 1947. Option D is incorrect as that did not happen until the partition of British India in 1948.

407. (A) Poland became part of the Russian Empire at the end of the 19th century and stayed that way until it was reborn at the Treaty of Versailles in 1919. Option C is incorrect because Croatia did not come into existence as an independent country until after the Balkan Wars of the 1990s. All other options are incorrect because they were states that existed prior to World War I.

408. (C) The Treaty of Versailles imposed harsh financial penalties on Germany. These proved quite difficult for Germany to meet and contributed to the economic problems in Germany in the 1920s, and thus, the conditions that allowed the Nazis to come to power in 1933. Option A is incorrect as it did nothing to Brest-Litovsk. Option B is incorrect as it had no effect on the breakout of World War II. Option D is incorrect because economic sanctions could occur without the treaty and would have had no effect on World War II, in any case.

409. (B) Lithuania was one of the Baltic countries that were part of the Russian Empire. It became independent following World War I and stayed that way for the interwar period. All other options are incorrect as they were independent countries or the head of empires before the war.

410. (A) This quote refers to major ethnic groups in Yugoslavia, which was formed after World War I. All other options are incorrect because there were no significant populations of these groups.

411. (B) Austria was required to pay reparations to the Allies as a result of the Treaty of St. Germain, signed after the Versailles Treaty on September 19, 1919. According to that treaty, Austria had 30 years to pay off its obligations, beginning in 1921. The treaty did not stipulate the exact amount the Austrians needed to pay, and ultimately, the Austrians paid nothing. Option C is incorrect as Germany had its military forces clearly limited by the treaty. All other options were specifically in the Treaty of Versailles.

412. (A) Alsace-Lorraine had been disputed between France and Germany for many years. It went to Germany after the Franco-Prussian War. However, it was returned to France after World War I. Option B is incorrect because Flanders has always been Belgian and has never been disputed. Options C and D are incorrect because both were always part of Germany and were never disputed, though the Rhineland was demilitarized after the war.

413. (D) World War I resulted in the destruction of the Ottoman Empire, which had once controlled the entire Middle East. After its dissolution, the Ottoman Empire was replaced by a number of protectorates. The modern-day country of Turkey was created in the area of Asia Minor and the city of Istanbul after World War I. Options A, B, and C are incorrect because they all lost territory as a result of World War I, although not nearly as much as the Ottoman Empire.

414. (C) Germany began to feel the impact of the spreading worldwide depression in the first quarter of 1928, a full year before its impact was felt in the United States. The Netherlands was impacted by the economic collapse in the fourth quarter of 1929, a few months after the United States. The United Kingdom (A) began to feel the depression in the first quarter of 1930, and France (B) was the last of the four, feeling the impact in the second quarter of 1930.

415. (D) Czechoslovakia was a relatively modern and democratic state in Eastern Europe. Option A is incorrect because Czechoslovakia was not the only member of the League of Nations in the area. Option B is incorrect because Czechoslovakia did not have a monarchy. Option C is incorrect because Czechoslovakia did not enjoy Soviet support at the time.

416. (B) Tito was the resistance leader in Yugoslavia who later became the leader of Yugoslavia. He had nothing to do with Italy. All other options correctly show the leaders of the countries they are paired with.

417. (D) The collapse of the Fourth Republic was precipitated by the controversy over Algeria. Algeria had been a French colony, but its independence movement created a constitutional crisis. Many white settlers in Algeria favored remaining part of the French union. Charles de Gaulle came out of retirement and forced the creation of a new constitution, with a much stronger executive. This was the beginning of the Fifth Republic. When Parliament voted for its own dissolution, this led to creation of the new constitution. Option A is incorrect because Germany was still partially occupied and was both politically and economically incapable of threatening any other country. Options B and C are incorrect because there was no economic collapse nor was the political crisis triggered by any economic reasons, including social welfare policy.

418. (A) The East German government created the Berlin Wall to prevent the growing tide of refugees that were leaving East Berlin for West Berlin. It was easy for East Germany residents to leave for the West by simply going to West Berlin, which was completely surrounded by East Germany. Option B is incorrect because building a wall would not prevent spies from entering East Berlin. Option C is incorrect because the wall was built eight years after the end of the Korean War, and the Korean War had nothing to do with the Berlin Wall. Option D is incorrect because German reunification was never formally disavowed by either the Soviet Union or the Western nations.

419. (D) After the war Berlin was located in the Soviet occupation zone of Germany. This led to many complications, including walls and separation schemes to keep people from crossing between Berlin and the rest of Germany. Option C is incorrect because there was no United Nations in Germany during the Cold War period. Options A and B are incorrect because they controlled the Western occupation zone of Germany along with the French, which was later united to become West Germany. West Germany constituted two-thirds of German territory until German reunification in 1989.

420. (B) The Iron Curtain got its name from a famous speech by Winston Churchill in 1946. He described areas of Eastern Europe controlled by the Soviet Union as being behind the Iron Curtain. This was an example of early Cold War rhetoric. Option A is incorrect because while Reagan derided the Iron Curtain and demanded the Berlin Wall be torn down, he did not invent the term "Iron Curtain." The other options are incorrect because they refer to Soviet leaders who would never use this term to describe the Cold War division between Communist and non-Communist. This would imply that their countries were prisons that people could not leave from.

421. (C) Yugoslavia, though a Communist state, was officially an independent country and asserted its independence soon after World War II. Marshal Tito, its leader, made a famous break with Moscow and Russian hegemony within Communism. All other options are incorrect because they correspond to Eastern European countries closely allied with the Soviet Union throughout the Cold War.

422. (A) The Sino-Soviet split that occurred in the 1950s created a division between the two most powerful Communist countries in the world. From then on Communism would cease to be a monolithic movement. Options B, C, and D are incorrect because although they occurred, Yugoslavia, Romania, and Albania are relatively small countries and did not present a serious threat to the Communist movement in general.

423. (A) Charles de Gaulle led France in an independent course between the Soviet Union and the United States at the time. De Gaulle would accept neither American dominance nor Soviet hegemony. He wasn't anti-Communist and sought to make France a power of its own. Option B is incorrect because the goal of de Gaulle was to take France out of military command of NATO in the 1960s, and therefore it could not be the leading member of the alliance. Option C is incorrect because de Gaulle distrusted West Germany and Britain and sought to keep Britain out of the common market. Option D is incorrect because de Gaulle was not a Communist and sought no alliance with the Warsaw Pact nations.

424. (B) The Security Council is composed of the five official victors of World War II—the United States, the Soviet Union, France, United Kingdom, and China. So Germany, the largest Western European state, is not a member of the Security Council.

425. (B) The Greek Civil War and Communist pressures on Turkey led to the Truman Doctrine, a formal declaration of support by the United States for countries being threatened by Communist takeover. The United States pledged its support for anti-Communist forces in small countries. Option A is incorrect because the Truman Doctrine was made in response to events in Greece and Turkey, and there had not yet been any Communist takeover in Vietnam. Option C is incorrect because there have been no Communist takeovers in West Germany or Italy. Option D is incorrect because there has been no Communist threat in Algeria.

426. (B) The European Economic Community had its origins in the European coal and steel community in the 1950s. This was a trade organization concerning steel producers at the time. All other options are incorrect because they have nothing directly to do with coal or steel production.

427. (D) The United Kingdom joined in the second round of membership in 1973 along with Denmark and Ireland. France (A), Germany (B), and Italy (C) were original members along with Belgium, Luxembourg, and the Netherlands.

428. (D) It was not until the Schengen Agreement in 1995 that citizens of member countries of what had become the European Union in 1993 under the Maastricht Treaty could travel freely within the union without passports. All three other answers were among the early accomplishments of the European Economic Community.

429. (D) Under Communism most ethnic differences were played down or suppressed. Ethnic groups were forced into greater political entities, which they may not have wanted to join. The entire Soviet Union was a nation of 16 different regions all held together by the national Soviet government in Moscow. When Communism fell, the nationalist feelings of various ethnic groups came to the surface, and this has resulted in violence and separatism in the post-Communist era. Option A is incorrect because the free-market economy has nothing to do with ethnic hatred. Option B is incorrect because ethnic and religious groups are not allowed complete freedom under Communism. Option C is incorrect because there has not been a great deal of nationalist violence in Eastern Europe, with the exception of the wars in Yugoslavia.

430. (C) Gandhi is known as a founder in the use of nonviolent opposition, and his use of it in India has become a model in other struggles. Option A is incorrect as it is the exact opposite of nonviolence, and Gandhi opposed such tactics as counterproductive. Options B and D are incorrect because though Gandhi did write, writing was not the main technique that he used.

431. (A) India was an important source of wealth and resources for the British Empire. This was proven again during the Second World War, when India provided thousands of troops and support for Britain during the conflict. Options B and D are incorrect. Although protests for independence continued through the war, protesters were careful not to disrupt the war effort. Option C is also incorrect. Although Britain did offer Dominion status to India in return for cooperation, Indian leaders turned the offer down, opting instead to push for full independence.

432. (C) The main problems of Russia during the war were food shortages, the collapse of the Russian war effort against Germany, and the lack of land for peasants. People demanded "Peace, Land, and Bread," a popular slogan of the time. Option A is incorrect because the majority of Russians were still peasants and therefore supported the agrarian, socialist-oriented Revolutionary Party (SR), not the Bolsheviks. Option B is incorrect because it was the soviets who were gaining power during this time at the expense of the Provisional government. Option D is incorrect because the Western democracies had supported the Provisional government and Lenin had promised to take Russia out of the war.

433. (B) Trotsky (and Lenin) feared that if the Communist Revolution did not break out in Western Europe, Russia would find itself isolated and surrounded by hostile capitalist regimes. Therefore, Trotsky favored organized support of workers' parties to create revolution abroad. Stalin believed this was impractical and wanted to oppose Trotsky politically in the ensuing power struggle, anyway. Option A is incorrect because it is exactly the opposite of Option B. Option C is incorrect as there was no party line; both leaders were endeavoring to make the party policy and that's what they were arguing about. Option D is incorrect because both believed that Russia would support Communism.

434. (A) These were the main demands of Russians in the summer and fall of 1917. The Russian people were exhausted by war and frustrated by czarist land ownership policies that favored nobles. Famine was ubiquitous in Russia, also. Option B is incorrect as it is the slogan of the French Revolution. Option C is also not a slogan, but a czarist policy. Option D is the Nazi policy of expansion.

435. (C) The Soviet Five-Year Plan was the method by which the Soviet Union embarked on a centrally planned economy. It was believed it would be more efficient than the supposed anarchy and duplication of capitalism. It was an exact plan for economic development over five years. Option A is incorrect as no such belief existed. Option B is incorrect because the Communist Party ran the state and was not separate from it. Option D is incorrect because under the Soviet Five-Year Plans, all economic resources were owned by the state.

436. (B) Marx theorized that it was necessary for a society to reach industrial capitalism for the circumstances to be right for a Socialist Revolution. Lenin had to come up with a way to explain how it was acceptable to create a Socialist Revolution in a country that was still predominantly rural. Option A is incorrect because urban workers helped overthrow the czar in 1917. Option C is incorrect as Marxism is clearly not religious, and the Russian masses were anything but atheistic. Option D is incorrect as there were many revolutionary groups in Russia who were either Marxist or well acquainted with Karl Marx.

437. (D) The Provisional government was what Karl Marx would call a bourgeois government, which supported civil liberties and private property. As such, workers and peasants were not represented. Option A is the exact opposite of Option D and is, therefore, incorrect. Option B is incorrect as this will not happen until November 1917. Option C is not correct as constitutional democrats ran the government.

438. (C) The NEP was Lenin's policy for the Russian economy to step back on recovery by allowing a small amount of private industry, while the government retained the "commanding heights" of heavy industrial production. It lasted throughout the 1920s. Option A is incorrect as it most closely follows the policy in the Soviet Union in the 1930s. Option B is incorrect because the Soviet Union was pretty much isolated during the 1920s. Option D is incorrect because there was never a policy to greatly increase consumer products during Soviet times.

439. (C) The Comintern (Communist International) was an organization that coordinated the activities of the Communist Party worldwide. The goal was to promote international proletarian revolutions, but in reality it became a foreign policy tool of the Communist Party of the Soviet Union. Option A is incorrect because the name of the Communist Party never changed from the one that Lenin gave it. Option B is incorrect because Comintern was not a secret organization. Option D is incorrect because the Soviet military never desired to acquire official colonies.

440. (C) Lenin believed that the only way a Communist Revolution would be successful would be if professional revolutionaries in a single unified party with clear structure, aims, and an official newspaper worked to bring it about. It was a much more specific plan than anything specified by Karl Marx. All other options were ideas of Karl Marx.

441. (D) The last organized opposition to Communist rule was the Kronstadt Rebellion of 1921. The rebellion was led by soldiers who initially were among the strongest supporters of the Bolshevik Revolution. As a result of the heavy-handed nature of Communist rule immediately after the revolution, the sailors withdrew their support for the Bolsheviks, calling for a government of "Soviets without Communists." Their rebellion was crushed by Red Army Civil War hero Mikhail Tukhachevsky. Options A, B, and C are incorrect because the civil war was still raging during these years and there was still some tolerance of non-Bolshevik groups.

442. (B) In 1918 Russia signed the Treaty of Brest-Litovsk, ceding the Baltic States and Poland to the Allied Powers. It also granted independence to Ukraine, Finland, and Georgia. In addition to massive territorial losses, the treaty also ceded vast amounts of mineral wealth. (C) and (D) involved post–World War I concessions by Hungary and Turkey.

443. (D) After the March 1917 revolution, Mensheviks supported and worked with the Constitutional Democrats who formed the Provisional government. Bolsheviks condemned such actions and opposed the Provisional government until its overthrow in November. Option A is incorrect as the Bolsheviks would want no such thing, as they were Marxists. Option B is incorrect as Mensheviks were still Socialists who were more inclined to agree with Bolsheviks on the goal of revolution, if not the means. Option C is incorrect as Mensheviks, if anything, were less ruthless than Bolsheviks.

444. (C) Czar Alexander II was not a figure in the Russian Revolution because he died almost 40 years before it occurred. Option A is incorrect because even though Rasputin was assassinated the year before the revolution, his influence on the royal family helped create the perception in Russia that the czar and his government were inept and incapable of leading the country. All other options are incorrect because they either fell from power (Kerensky) or rose to power (Lenin) because of the revolution.

445. (C) Hitler was ideologically opposed to Bolshevism. He also believed that the German people were a great race that needed a large territory to settle. This territory would be obtained from the vast expanse of the Soviet Union. Option A is incorrect because Japan was allied with Germany and was much too far away from Europe to be any kind of threat to Germany. Option B is incorrect because Hitler had already defeated the French and, if anything, a war with Russia would detract from his efforts against the British. Option D is incorrect because, though Hitler employed a racist ideology, he did not seek to exterminate the Slavic population as he did with the Jews.

446. (C) Germany used Belgium to attack France twice. In World War I Germans attacked France through Belgium in order to be able to get to Paris quickly. In World War II the Germans attacked France through Belgium in order to go around the Maginot Line. Option A is incorrect because the military push in the Balkans that occurred during World War II was not until 1941, two years after the war had begun. Option B is incorrect because Germany was not allied with Japan during World War I. Option D is incorrect because the Germans did not respect the rights of American vessels during either war.

447. (D) Southern France between 1940 and 1942 was governed by Marshall Henri Petain. The capital was at Vichy, which is why it was called Vichy France. It was a puppet state of the Germans. Option A is incorrect because no part of France was prosperous during this time. Option B is incorrect because Free French was a resistance movement under Charles de Gaulle headquartered in London, not an area of France. Option C is incorrect because Georges Clemenceau was not a figure in French politics until after the war.

448. (B) The Sudetenland, an area of western Czechoslovakia inhabited by German speakers, was cleared for takeover by the Germans at the Munich Conference of 1938. Many considered it to be an appeasement of Hitler. Option A is incorrect because people of the Saarland had voted to reunite with Germany in 1935. Option C is incorrect because Austria had already been annexed by Nazi Germany earlier that year. Option D is incorrect because Poland would be invaded by Nazi Germany only in September 1939, which would begin World War II.

449. (D) The Germans perfected the blitzkrieg, the concept of "lightning war." This was an overwhelming use of force in a methodical and organized fashion to quickly conquer territory and subdue defenders. This led to the quick German conquest of Poland and France. Option A is incorrect because the German technology in World War II, at least at the start of the war, was not significantly superior to British and French technology. Option B is incorrect because there was no clear French insistence on endlessly fighting, and the French command surrendered relatively soon after it became clear that the cause was lost. Option C is incorrect because Britain did not invade Norway until after the initial German victories.

450. (A) Radar was a key invention of World War II. It enabled the British to see exactly where the German planes that were going to bomb England were coming from. It significantly reduced the effectiveness of the German bombing and caused great losses of German planes. It is probably the main reason why Hitler was forced to give up on the Battle of Britain. Option B is incorrect because V-2 rockets were not used until the end of the war, and they played no significant role in the outcome of the war. Option C is incorrect because the Germans, not the British, used

Tiger tanks. Option D is incorrect because, while sonar was widely used during World War II, it had no significant effect on the Battle of Britain.

451. (A) The main issue during the Potsdam Conference of July 1945 was the future of the Eastern European countries that had just been conquered by the Soviet Union and whether or not they would be free. Elections were one of the main issues being discussed. Option B is incorrect because no discussion of future military forces or their limits were established at the Potsdam Conference. Option C is incorrect because there was no discussion about compensation for the Holocaust, and it would have involved more than Russian Jews. Option D is incorrect because the Soviet Union was already going to be a founding member of the United Nations.

452. (C) The turning point of the eastern campaign during World War II was the Battle of Stalingrad. The Russians stopped the German advance at Stalingrad, and the Germans began a long retreat that lasted until the end of the war. Option A is incorrect because the Germans were not defeated by the Soviets in Poland until the last year of the war. The Germans were already in retreat. Option B is incorrect because there was no major Soviet theater of operations in Iran nor were there any Germans in Iran. Option D is incorrect because there was no German mutiny at Leningrad.

453. (B) The center of Nazi ideology was racism. All races were put on a hierarchy, the lowest being Jews and right above them the Slavs. Accordingly, the Nazi occupation in Eastern Europe and the western Soviet Union was quite harsh. Even people inclined to sympathize with the Nazis were soon alienated after that. Option A is incorrect because there was no difference between Eastern and Western Europe with regard to their inclination to collaborate with the Germans. Option C is incorrect because while American and British soldiers may have been treated more humanely, that was not a significant difference in the occupation. Option D is incorrect because Jews suffered even more in the East than they did in the West during the Holocaust.

454. (C) Nazi war criminals would classically defend their actions by saying that they were just following the orders of their superiors. Therefore, they could bear no responsibility for war crimes. Option A is incorrect because they were being prosecuted for war crimes and genocide against civilians, not crimes that occurred in the course of war. Option B is incorrect because it would not have cleared them of war crimes. Option D is incorrect because they did not claim this, and it would not result in their being excused for war crimes.

455. (C) The Vichy government was a conservative Catholic government that passively cooperated with the Nazis. Option A is incorrect because it was a paternalistic, authoritarian regime and would clearly not be described as socialistic or democratic. Option B is clearly incorrect because the Vichy government was a Catholic and conservative government. Option D is incorrect because Vichy France was not liberal nor did it seek to expand anywhere.

456. (B) At Yalta, the Allies decided to divide Germany into zones of control by the winning powers. The goal was to eventually reunite the different sections of Germany. Option A is incorrect because there was a clear plan coming out of Yalta concerning what to do with Germany after the war. Option C is incorrect because the French were going to be included as one of the occupying powers, which would make three, not two, blocs. Option D is incorrect because the Marshall Plan was not organized until after the war. The Marshall Plan was also a response to the postwar domination of Eastern Europe by the Soviet Union.

457. (D) European countries did not have an open-borders policy in the 20th century. Options A (decolonization), B (the importation of large numbers of non-European soldiers and temporary workers during the wars), and C (the demand for laborers after WWII) were all contributing factors to the rise of immigration during that century.

458. (B) Churchill was referring to the efforts of the Royal Air Force to defend Britain against the Nazi bombing during the Battle of Britain. The efforts of the Royal Air Force to protect the country prevented many deaths. All other options refer to events that occurred after Churchill spoke those words. Churchill's words became famous and were used in British propaganda soon after he uttered them.

459. (A) France's immigration policy was considered to be an economic success. Options B and C are incorrect because in the late 20th century, lack of integration of some of its immigrants had caused sharp conflicts among France's diverse population. Option D is incorrect because despite the tightening of immigration regulations, the number of immigrants entering the country was continuing to rise.

460. (C) Britain was the victor at the Battle of El Alamein, which ended the Africa campaign. The Germans and Italians tried to capture North Africa and the Middle East, thereby threatening English shipping to India and the Middle East. The British victory put an end to this threat and brought to a close the entire African theater of war. Option A is incorrect because the Germans lost the battle. Option B is incorrect because the Soviet Union was not even involved in the battle. Option D is incorrect because even though Americans were present in some parts of the African theater, they did not take part in this battle.

461. (D) The Soviet Union was not present at the Munich Conference and saw the Munich Conference as a trial. The Soviet Union had a strategic alliance with Czechoslovakia, and the Munich Conference led to the dismemberment of Czechoslovakia and its eventual annexation by Germany. All other options are incorrect because they were parties present at the conference and agreed to the treaty that resulted from it. In that treaty, the Sudetenland, which was German-speaking, went to Germany and the rest of Czechoslovakia soon after that.

462. (B) Neville Chamberlain was the British prime minister at the time, and he famously came back to England after the Munich Conference and proclaimed "peace in our time." This was widely seen as a weak approach to Hitler and a glaring example of the failed policy of appeasement to Hitler. Chamberlain believed he had avoided war with Hitler and Germany, which he did, but only for a year. All of the other options are incorrect. Also, Churchill saw the folly of the appeasement strategy and did not support the Munich Conference at all. Stalin did not even take part in the Munich Conference nor did Roosevelt.

463. (C) The strategy of island-hopping concerns a way to reach Japan with the minimum loss of time and life. Accordingly, the Americans attacked smaller, less heavily defended islands as a way to break the Japanese supply lines. This caused larger Japanese bases to be cut off and, therefore, allowed to "wither and die." Option A is incorrect because it is the exact opposite of the strategy proposed by island-hopping. Too much time, money, material, and men would be used if all of the islands were conquered. Option B is similarly not correct because too much time and money would be used to conquer the heavily fortified islands. Option D is incorrect because, while the air force was used extensively, it could not be used to wipe out military bases all by itself.

464. (A) The vast majority of the immigrants to the United Kingdom in the 20th century were from former colonies of the country. Options B and C are incorrect because very few of the immigrants in the United Kingdom were from other European countries. Option D is incorrect because NATO was primarily a tool for keeping peace, not for influencing migration patterns.

465. (C) After reunification, the share of foreign population in East Germany was below one percent, so reunification had very little impact on the country's migration patterns. Option A is true as the majority of migrants in Germany at that time came from Turkey. Other contributors were Yugoslavia, Greece, and Italy. Options B and D are also true. In the early 1990s, Germany's population was more than 20 percent foreign-born, and more than 12 million immigrants settled in Germany after World War II.

466. (C) France was especially welcoming to Moroccans, Algerians, and other citizens of its former colonies. As a result, many of its immigrants originated from those countries. Option A is not true because although France's economy thrived during that period, it was not necessarily stronger than all of the other economies in Europe. Option B is not true because other European countries, such as Spain and Italy, were as close or closer to North Africa than France was. Option D is also not true as France did not have a significant immigrant population from communist countries.

467. (D) In the late 20th century, Western Europe struggled to find ways to integrate large immigrant populations into its nations' various cultures. Options A, B, and C are all false. Immigration countered falling birthrates and supplied a workforce. Immigration to Western Europe was on the rise and policies to curtail it were being implemented in many countries. Immigration to Western Europe was creating a racially diverse continent.

468. (A) EU nationals are free to work and live in any EU country and are given free access to its labor markets. Option B is incorrect because member countries cannot impose quotas. Option C is incorrect because the law applied only to EU citizens. Option D is incorrect because EU citizens were subject to the laws of the country in which they were living.

469. (C) The turning point of the eastern front turned out to be the Battle of Stalingrad in 1942 and 1943. After that the Germans were forced to begin a long retreat back to Germany. Likewise, the major naval defeat of the Japanese at the Battle of Midway was a crippling setback for their overall plans for the war and began a slow retreat back to the Japanese home islands. Option A is incorrect because millions of Russians and other Soviet citizens died during World War II, and the Soviet military leadership was quite profligate in its attitude toward human life. Option B is incorrect because the Maginot Line was built between World War I and World War II and yet proved completely ineffective as the Germans simply bypassed it by going through the Netherlands and Belgium. Option D is incorrect because military intelligence managed to decode both German and Japanese encrypted messages. This ability proved critical to many World War II battles.

470. (D) Clement Atlee's postwar Labour government undertook a social democratic legislative program after the war. Accordingly, it strove to build housing for common people and, therefore, undertook a major housing program. His administration had strong support from British trade unions, and part of his program was for the government to take over certain key industries. It also embarked on a large expansion of the British welfare state. Therefore, all options are correct.

471. (D) The Marshall Plan was a way to create prosperity and stability in Europe in the face of a possible Communist takeover. By rebuilding Europe, the Marshall Plan would dampen the allure of Communism and also provide a market for American goods. Options A and B are incorrect because there was no requirement placed on countries to participate in the Marshall Plan. Any country in Europe was officially invited to join. Option C is incorrect because the Marshall Plan was seen as a great success by the time it was over.

472. (B) Alexander Dubcek, the leader of Czechoslovakia in 1968, sought a liberalization of the Communist regime in Czechoslovakia. This was ended when the Soviet Union invaded Czechoslovakia and reestablished an orthodox Communist regime in 1968. Option A is incorrect because the Prague Spring had nothing to do with any green revolution in Eastern Europe. Likewise, Option C is incorrect as there was no agricultural aspect to the Prague Spring and no drought in 1968. Option D is incorrect because there was no great flowering of Czech literature as Czechoslovakia became a Communist satellite soon after World War II.

473. (A) Gorbachev was not a capitalist, but he saw what was wrong in the Soviet economy and tried to restructure it in a Socialist manner. Perestroika was the economic counterpart to glasnost, which was a new political openness in Soviet society. Option B is incorrect because Gorbachev did not try to create a three-person directorate or create any major change in Soviet political institutions. Option C is incorrect because Gorbachev never sought to abolish the KGB. Option D is incorrect because Gorbachev sought no drastic political restructuring at first; perestroika moved along gradually.

474. (A) The Khrushchev era was known as the "thaw." Khrushchev ended severe Stalinist repression and freed large numbers of political prisoners. Option B is incorrect because although Khrushchev created new agricultural programs, these did not create big advances in agricultural production. Option C is incorrect as the Soviet Union never sought to join NATO. Option D is incorrect because Khrushchev tried to increase the amount of consumer goods but did not actually try to create a consumer economy.

475. (C) Despite the encouragement of American broadcasts, there was no explicit military assistance to revolutionaries in anti-Communist rebellions in Eastern Europe. As a result, all protests against Communist rule during most of the Cold War were crushed. Option B is incorrect because all Soviet bloc eastern satellites were expected to remain loyal to the USSR during this time and to closely follow the economy prescribed by Moscow. Option A is incorrect because this is also covered in Option C. Option D is incorrect because there were future protests against Communist rule after the Polish and Hungarian uprisings of 1956.

476. (C) The Cuban missile crisis was seen as a capitulation of the Soviet Union to the demands of the United States. The United States demanded that the Soviets bring back missiles that had been installed in Cuba, 90 miles away from the American coast. Even though the United States promised to remove missiles from Turkey aimed at the Soviet Union, this was not revealed until many years later, and it seemed as though Khrushchev had backed down, which cost him domestic support. Option A is incorrect because de-Stalinization was a popular policy within the Soviet Union and had created a more open atmosphere. Option B is incorrect because most of the Soviet Union had supported the way the Hungarian Revolution had been suppressed by Soviet troops. Option D is incorrect because the Bay of Pigs was an invasion of Cuba by Cuban exiles, and it probably would have been supported by Soviet people.

477. (D) The Brezhnev Doctrine stated that Communist countries or countries within the Soviet sphere of influence could not stop being Communist nor could they leave the Soviet sphere of influence. Option A is incorrect because while the Brezhnev Doctrine might affect Communist countries in Southeast Asia, it affected all countries within the Soviet sphere of influence. Option B is incorrect because the Brezhnev Doctrine did not apply to NATO countries, which were by definition outside of the Soviet sphere of influence. Option C is incorrect because the Brezhnev Doctrine affected countries outside of the Soviet Union, as it was a foregone conclusion that Soviet republics could never become non-Soviet.

478. (C) The overall competition between the Soviet Union and the West concerned the competition over political and economic systems. Option A is incorrect because the Soviet Union was given a very prominent role in the postwar division of Germany, beginning in 1945. Option B is incorrect because religion did not play a significant role in the conflict. Option D is incorrect because the border between Poland and Germany was pretty clearly established after the war and has not changed since.

479. (B) In 1982 Argentina attacked and conquered the Falkland Islands, a small archipelago of islands a few hundred miles east of Argentina that has been administered by Britain for the past 200 years. When Margaret Thatcher, prime minister of Britain at the time, sent a military force to take the islands back, the British people rallied to her support in a wave of nationalism. In the following weeks Britain successfully won the Falkland Islands back from Argentina after a short war.

480. (A) Nationalization of industries would be the exact opposite of Thatcherism. Thatcherism could be described as a policy of clear confidence in the free market, which is the opposite of nationalization of industries. All other options are incorrect because destroying the power of labor unions, reducing taxes, reducing government spending, and close partnership with the United States were all pillars of Margaret Thatcher's policies.

481. (C) Lech Walesa served as president of Poland from 1990 to 1995. Angela Merkel (A), though born in Hamburg, grew up in East Germany near Berlin after her father, a Lutheran minister, was posted there. She became chancellor of a united Germany in 2005. Vaclav Havel, novelist, dissident, and intellectual, was the last president of Czechoslovakia and the first president of the Czech Republic from 1993 to 2003. Dalia Grybauskaite (D), known as Lithuania's "Iron Lady," was born in Soviet-occupied Vilnius and became president of her native country in 2009.

482. (D) The Catholic Church served as a vanguard for the Solidarity movement in Poland. The Solidarity movement in Poland was closely allied with the Catholic Church during the late 1970s and early 1980s. The church strongly supported Solidarity and used its protected place in society, even during Communist times, as a sort of sanctuary for the Solidarity movement and Solidarity figures. Option A is incorrect because the Communist Party controlled the Polish Parliament. Option B is incorrect because while members of the peasantry may have supported Solidarity, it is not an institution and is not what gave the Solidarity movement support and protection. Option C is incorrect because the Polish army did not support Solidarity movements during its heyday.

483. (C) In 1991 Slovenia and Croatia declared their independence from the Federal Republic of Yugoslavia. The Yugoslav Republic, made up mainly of Serbs, tried to prevent them from leaving. Serbs, living in Croatia, tried to break away from Croatia. Soon the region was embroiled in civil war, which devolved into all-out ethnic cleansing vendettas. Option A is incorrect because although Croatia eventually applied for NATO membership, this was not the cause of the 1991 war and did not happen until many years afterward. Option B is incorrect because although there was severe fighting between Bosnian Muslims and Serbs in Bosnia, this also did not happen until after 1991. Option D is incorrect because there were no Croatian, Slovenian, and Bosnian attacks on Serbia.

484. (B) Czechoslovakia peacefully broke into two different ethnic enclaves in 1993, the Czech Republic and the Slovak Republic. This was done via a simple vote of the Czechoslovak Parliament. Option A is incorrect because Czechoslovakia did eventually join the European Community and NATO, but not for a number of years. Option C is incorrect because Czechoslovakia did not take sides in that Balkan war. Option D is incorrect because while Czechoslovakia allowed more local autonomy for ethnic minorities, the nation divided into two main ethnic groups, Czechs and Slovaks.

485. (D) The first space satellite launched in history was created by the Soviet Union. The Soviets beat the Americans to this achievement, and it was a particularly impressive achievement seen across the world. Option A is incorrect because although the Soviets created many large and impressive dams, the dam on the Volga River is not the world's largest, nor was it at the time. Option B is incorrect because the construction of the gulag network of concentration camps was not a scientific or engineering achievement. Option C is incorrect because, while the Soviet Union created high-quality fighter planes, so did many other countries and the American ones were usually considered to be of better quality.

486. (C) Guerrilla wars became numerous in the 1960s and 1970s because of the continuation of national independence movements and the realization that traditional styles of war might lead eventually to nuclear conflict. Therefore, guerrilla and asymmetrical types of warfare became more numerous during the nuclear age, not less. Option A is incorrect because mutually assured destruction is the theory that nuclear war will eventually lead to the complete destruction of both combatants and, therefore, is not an acceptable form of warfare. Option B is incorrect because nuclear weapons became more numerous in the nuclear age, and eventually proliferated to a number of countries. Option D is incorrect because nuclear weapons are expensive and require delivery systems such as long-range bombers and missiles, which have consequences for national economies.

487. (C) Impressionism was a 19th-century artistic movement. All other options are 20th-century artistic movements.

488. (B) As of 2016, women were still not allowed to serve as priests in the Catholic church.

489. (B) Slovakia refused to accept any Muslim refugees and would only accept a limited number of Christian refugees. Option A is incorrect because immigration concerns were a leading cause of the Brexit vote. Options C and D are wrong because Bulgaria did build a fence and Hungary did refuse to accept refugees.

490. (C) Finland was the first European country to grant women the right to vote. This was given in 1906 as a result of the General Strike of 1905 as well as some other political factors in that country. Options B and D are incorrect as women were granted the right to vote in Norway in 1913 and in Denmark two years later. Option A is also incorrect. Poland gave women the vote in 1918, two years before women in the United States would be granted that right.

491. (A) The Representation of the People Act, passed in 1918, granted women the right to vote, although there were age (minimum 30 years old) and other restrictions.

492. (D) Women in many countries were mobilized for the war effort, freeing men to fight. Even after the war, though most women had to leave their new jobs, newly acquired suffrage and experience in a much larger number of work roles gave women an enhanced status and opened up many areas of employment to them, whereas before they had been limited to such jobs as domestic servants. Option A is incorrect as there were still plenty of male supervisors. Option B is incorrect because women were often used during the war for heavy manual labor. Option C is incorrect because suffrage was usually granted after the war, not before.

493. (A) Women in Western Europe in the second half of the 20th century have achieved much greater equality with men in the workforce than ever before. Women participate in equal numbers with men in many occupations. Option B is incorrect because although women have made great strides in the workforce, they still do not have wage equality with men. Option C is incorrect because women in Western Europe live longer than men; this is true of almost all Western European countries. Option D is incorrect because family size in Europe has gotten much smaller over the past 40 years, and some European countries do not even have enough children to replace their populations.

494. (D) Portugal did not grant women the vote until 1976. Switzerland (C) extended the franchise to women in 1971. French women (A) gained the vote in 1944 and Italy (B) gave women the vote in 1945.

495. (A) India became an independent country in 1947 and Elizabeth did not ascend to the throne until 1952. As Britain's longest-serving monarch (D) who has witnessed many of the profound changes of the last half of the 20th century and into the 21st century, Queen Elizabeth has been credited with building a strong Commonwealth of Nations (B). The organization, formerly known as the British Commonwealth, is made up of 53 member states with ties to the United Kingdom. Many of the countries are former colonies within the old British Empire. She also played a pivotal role in encouraging peace in Ireland when she expressed support for the Good Friday Peace Agreement (C) by meeting with Mary McAleese, President of Ireland, in 1998.

496. (A) The resolution issued in 2006 by the European Parliament called on member states to protect transgender, lesbian, gay, and bisexual people from hate speech, violence, or any type of discrimination. It also called on them to grant equal rights to gay and lesbian couples. Options B and D are incorrect, although there were immigration concerns during that time and some of the member states had experienced terrorist attacks. Option C is incorrect as well, although the European Parliament has passed various resolutions upholding women's rights.

497. (D) European countries would grapple with the issue of multiculturalism in a variety of ways as various waves of immigration swept over the continent in the 50 years following World War II and into the 21st century, as each surge of immigration added to community pressures and challenges.

498. (D) With a burgeoning economy and a lack of able-bodied industrial workers, West Germany launched a guest worker program in 1960. When the Berlin Wall was built, shutting off access to cheaper East German labor, the program was expanded, and by 1964 one million foreign workers had settled in West Germany.

499. (D) Both sides of the divided Germany needed workers to rebuild the industrial sector after World War II and as the booming 1960s raised demand for workers. Between 1966 and 1989, on the eve of the fall of the Soviet Union, half a million immigrants from Vietnam, Poland, Mozambique, and elsewhere immigrated to East Germany.

500. (D) France legalized homosexual acts between adults in 1791, 212 years before the United States, which did not legalize homosexual acts until 2003. Poland (A) legalized the activity in 1932, Germany (B) in 1969, and Russia (C) in 1993.

NOTES

NOTES

NOTES